Serving Time Together

Serving Time Together

A Correspondence of Hearts

Ruth Sanders and Martin Forrest

ELEMENT
Rockport, Massachusetts • Shaftesbury, Dorset

© 1992 Ruth Sanders

Published in the U.S.A. in 1992 by
Element, Inc.
42 Broadway, Rockport, MA 01966

Published in Great Britain in 1992 by
Element Books Limited
Longmead, Shaftesbury, Dorset

Designed by Roger Lightfoot
Cover design by Max Fairbrother
Cover Illustration by Kate Elkin
Phototypeset by Intype, London
Printed and bound in the U.S.A. by
Edwards Brothers, Inc.

British Library Cataloguing in Publication data available

Library of Congress Catalog Card Number available

ISBN 1–85230–340–9

Credits
Quotation from *The Notebooks of Paul Brunton*, Volume 1: *Perspectives*.
Copyright © 1984 by the Paul Brunton Philosophic Foundation
and Larson Publications. Reprinted by permission.

Quotation from *The Great Initiates* by Edward Schuré. Copyright ©
1961 by St. George Books. Reprinted by permission of Rudolf
Steiner Publications, Inc.

Contents

Editor's Note

Ruth and Martin want this book to accomplish two goals: they want it to communicate the important ideas that contributed to Martin's transformation, and Martin and Ruth's growth. They also want the book to portray certain aspects of life on earth at this time in evolution, especially life in prison in America.

Since Martin continues to live within the prison system, the publisher has chosen to change the names of both authors in order to protect him. Although Ruth and Martin both initially indicated that they preferred not to publish under assumed names, they have graciously acceded to Element's discretion in this matter. In addition, all references to the prison where Martin is incarcerated have been edited for his protection.

Ruth and Martin wrote often, sometimes daily, and the abundance of material necessitated significant editing by Ruth. Many letters have been condensed, excerpted, or completely omitted. Only rarely has grammatical presentation been changed in the hope that this book would retain the charm and quality of this very special, loving, caring exchange.

An Introduction by Ruth Sanders

How amazing it is to look back over seventy-five years of an active, changeful life and find myself having a first book published. One could say that the word *change* is the key to this life. Change does not mean unsteadiness; I have been as steady and as true to one thing as anyone can possibly be. I had chosen an inner path and followed it wherever it took me. And it took me to many different places, many occupations, meetings with many different people, travel to Europe, three husbands. Each change was a new step in the progress along the path.

To Rudolf Steiner—philosopher, teacher, scientist, spiritual scientist—I owe most grateful thanks. He has been my teacher from the time I was thirty. We never met, for he died when I was eight years old. I was able, however, to learn from the vast heritage he left behind in the form of printed materials and the work of his followers in many different fields. It was never dogma, nor imitation, but only (as he taught) by taking his indications and testing them, seeking truth as I could prove it for myself. My struggling steps in growth were enhanced, and some even made possible, because of his teachings.

My path took me to Missouri, not terribly far from the place I grew up on a farm in Indiana. I stayed in Missouri nine years, and here I received my training in ultimate aloneness and deeper unity at the same time. Here I got my exercise in coming in contact with the deepest inner self, that one who is different from and yet united with everything and everyone in the world. And it was here that I made contact with Martin.

At that time, arthritis made it impossible for me to be physically active, and so to give me something worthwhile to do, I took some names of prisoners who wanted to correspond with people outside of prison from the "Connections" page in *Sojourners* magazine. With many names on the list, how could one choose? In the end I picked several names and sent along a copy of a self-published book—a kind of spiritual biography. I would not have been surprised had no one responded. However, some did, and that's how the meaningful and loving exchange between Martin and myself began.

What I had to say came to life in my letters to Martin, perhaps because for the first time someone wanted to hear it. Martin could recognize that it was from a certain knowledge that I spoke and not just opinion and drew from me, like the hungry soul that he was and is, those things that had brought about my own transformation. For almost the first time in his life, Martin wanted to listen. And sometimes he answered, "Yes, I know that too." I told him to always question, investigate, and test everything for himself until he knew it in his own heart and being. If he did that, then it would become meaningful for him and would work in him without his even uttering a word.

But most important of all, I think, is the magic of our coming together again, an elderly white woman and a young black man from such different backgrounds who grew up in such different ways and circumstances. Yet in soul we are as one— we share a love that glimpses of the past show us has lasted more than ten thousand years. That love continues and grows and knows no barriers. A wonderful relationship arranged, of course, by the angels. How else could two people so far apart in every way meet again and renew an old, so very close bond and share a deep, so very deep love that transcends all else.

An Introduction by Martin Forrest

At this writing I am confined to a twelve-by-eight-foot cell, twenty-four hours a day, every day. It has been this way for the last four years, with the exception of a two-month respite at a mental hospital. I have been in this prison system for ten years now. According to the prison administrators, I am ranked among the most dangerous and uncontrollable prisoners at this state prison. For this reason I am restrained and deprived of any activities outside of this cell. I am on a wing that is above the death chambers and the electric chair.

I have a different opinion of myself than the somewhat exaggerated one of my captors. However, in an attempt to be honest, I cannot fully disagree with their limited view of me. Like anyone else, when threatened, I am apt to be dangerous, and I have been known to rebel against established blind authority. My imprisonment is evidence of that.

The contents of this book were not originally intended for publication. As you will see, it is comprised of personal and intimate letters between two people. It started out as a correspondence between an elderly lady and an angry, repressed, and frustrated prisoner. It has proven to be the most challenging and the highest learning experience in my life. And, more than anything else, it has proven to be the most loving. Only because of this deep mutual love between us has the relationship been a miraculous success. My experience with Ruth has taught me that when love is the foundation of a relationship, truth, honesty, and goodwill naturally follow. I am gradually learning to view my prison condition, and the things that may come to me in the future, with equanimity. Blind anger and ignorance of the things life has presented to me are slowly being overcome. After being practically raised in the prison houses of America, I had firmly convinced myself that America's white-ruled society and life had failed me miserably.

This was my standard cop-out for all of my shortcomings and self-induced miseries. It has taken many years of painful experiences, many hours of grueling self-analysis, honesty, and courage to come to the indubitable truth that life only fails a man when he fails himself.

I am still in my early and fundamental stages of learning. Read along with me, and in our reading together, perhaps we can contribute to our mutual growth process on this path of life.

CHAPTER 1

Meeting and Getting Acquainted

August 8, 1988

Dear friend,

Today I received a book called *Should It Make Sense?* I don't know what inspired you to send it, but I am sure glad you did. It is truly a godsend. This is the type of literature that I enjoy reading over and over. I can never thank you enough for your consideration and thoughtfulness in sending me these enlightening words. I am presently unable to purchase anything, but if you have any literature that you can afford to send, it will be very much appreciated.

It is a blessing to know that people such as yourself are willing to help others without looking for anything in return. You see, my opinion of people was starting to get really negative until you came along. I would like to say thanks for giving me this lift.

I will be very delighted to hear from you again.

Love yah!
Martin

———

August 11, 1988

Dear Martin,

I took your name from the "Connections" page in the *Sojourners* magazine. I had looked at the prisoner list, wondering how to pick a name at random when there is no indication of who might be at the other end. There are a great many reasons for being in prison, and though most are criminals, Gandhi also went to prison, so one never knows. That does not matter. For me it was a question of finding someone compatible. Each experience has something to teach us, and when one is older, it is being a continual student that helps to give us youth. I thought if I sent my book, impersonally, it might bring a response from the kind of person with whom it might be easier and more interesting to have an exchange. I am sending another book, and you may have any of the others that I publish from the enclosed list. There is also a bookmark, handwoven by me, to go with the books.

If you want to continue writing letters, I will try to keep up with them.

Love yah, too,
Ruth

———————

August 15, 1988

Dear Ruth,

Your letter and reading material were received in good faith and very much appreciated. The stories you sent are very touching. They moved me in a way that I cannot put into words; all of them are beautiful. Thank you.

I have been incarcerated for six years now. I was sentenced to twenty. Unlike Gandhi I am of the criminal element. I practically have been raised in institutions for delinquents. Do you think that in this way I am paying dues for something that happened in one of my past lives? I do not necessarily see my being incarcerated as punishment because it has afforded me the chance to meet people such as yourself.

Your bookmark is beautiful, and I will cherish it always. I am glad and fortunate that you picked my name from the magazine. I consider myself blessed to have the privilege of befriending someone such as yourself. I would love to continue writing to you. Keep up your beautiful work.

Love yah!
Martin

———————

August 19, 1988

Dear Martin,

I was very touched by your remark that being incarcerated affords you the chance to meet certain people. It was an answer similar to one I once gave to some handicapped children. I was working in a home in Scotland where there was a rather large turnover of help, and I was leaving after about three months. The children and I were feeling very sad about parting. I told them that since they were not able to go out into the world, the world was coming to them, and I pointed out that people were coming there from all over the world for training.

The first two lessons I learned there were that the ill and disturbed are no different from the so-called "normal" people except in degree; and that though I had gone there thinking I would help them, it was I who was being helped and taught— I was being given so very much. With the ill, as with very young children in general, there is no subterfuge, fakery, and so on. They are just what they are. My own tendency to be that way does not go over well in the world, but I preserve and guard the right to be just plainly my real self as much as possible. So, I was comfortable with the children in the institution.

After leaving Scotland, I continued my studies in Germany for about two years. Life—destiny—has led me to have a great many different experiences and to move about a great deal. I think the eight years here in Missouri is the longest period I have been in one place since childhood and that was very long ago; I'm on the way to seventy-two now. The feeling that was strongest as I approached seventy was great surprise, and that feeling is still there.

To answer your question about "paying dues for something in a previous life," various things are possible, and of course, unless one is clairvoyant and can actually "see" it, one doesn't know. Besides that possibility, one can be sharing in the events of the times, and one can be in training for future work in the world. I remember reading something from Dr. Steiner about a genius having to have gone through a life of being mentally handicapped.

I would be interested to know more about you—your age, background—anything you feel like writing about. What about your life in prison? What are your days like, your cell? Do you work there?

I spend a lot of time alone these days, partly because I am no longer able to be physically active and also, being an oddball, I don't have a lot of exchange with the local people. The neighbors are friendly, and I know there would be help if needed. That is very comforting.

I am impressed by your attitude with regard to being in prison. I suppose when you have spent such a long time there it must be a way of life. For many people the problems may be just as intense, or perhaps in some ways worse, in the outside world. What is most important—growing, learning— one can do anywhere, so, you have just given me a fresh outlook about it.

I am enclosing a few odds and ends of things you may find interesting. They are of no special choice, just things on hand. They need not be returned. The two poems are mine.

I am privileged to have made a connection with you. Do you mind my sharing your letters, or parts, with friends?

Love,
Ruth

———

August 23, 1988

Dear Ruth,

May this letter find you in the best of health, spirit, and mood. Your latest reading material is very much appreciated. Thank you. Your poems are very touching, especially "Ode to Joy," which touches something within me that hasn't been touched before.

I never really took time to find out where I was born, but I believe it was in the south. During my elementary years, I went to school in New Jersey. I completed the seventh and eighth grades in Lake Placid. My parents and I agreed that it would be better for me to quit school after the eighth grade to help take care of the other kids—there were ten in all, three boys and seven girls. I'm the third oldest. The youngest child, a boy, died from crib death. About a year after I quit school, I got into some trouble with the law. After a couple of more incidents with the law, I was sent to live with a foster family. The lady in charge of my new home told me the only reason she was accepting me was because of the money she would be making. I felt very unwanted, so after about eight months, I left. I tried making it on my own, but failed. As destiny would have it, I ended up back in the hands of the law. You know, the more I think about it the more I'm convinced that in a very mysterious way I was rescued instead of being arrested. The community was infested with drugs, lies, deceit, and death. But for the grace of God I never could have come this far.

I have been in and out of institutions, mental and correctional, since I was fourteen years of age. I am now twenty-eight years old and thanks to people like yourself, I am beginning to realize my spiritual self. Isn't it beautiful? We share similar problems as far as being ourselves, especially since I am just beginning to realize my true self in this type of environment. I am open to all advice and suggestions concerning this matter.

I have been incarcerated ten years this time for armed robbery, doing twenty years on the charge. At the moment, I am on close management confinement for an indefinite period of time. I had a physical confrontation with the guards here that resulted in my having an operation on my left wrist and then being placed in confinement. Problems like that are an everyday occurrence around here. I could have prevented the situation from happening, but I chose not to.

Do you think that there is a positive and negative occurrence to every given situation? I really can't explain why I chose to feed their sickness other than my stubbornness and temper at the time. Anyway, I am working very hard on them. I'm locked in this cell twenty-four hours a day except for three times a week when I am allowed out to take a five-minute shower. It is very hot in here, but I know I am doing better than most people because I am yearning to know God. When I meditate on God, my problems and troubles are forgotten.

You know I feel happy and at peace after receiving your letter and just sitting here writing to you. I am honored that you think so much of my letters to want to share them with someone. By all means, please feel free to do so. Thank you.

There is so much beauty in your work until I'm amazed at how much I've been missing. So, my dearest Ruth, you see my reasoning for considering myself fortunate to have met you? I am revealing things to you that I wouldn't dream of telling the average soul, that's how comfortable I feel with you. Take care!

Love,
Martin

─────────

August 26, 1988

Dear Martin,

I'm glad you liked "Ode to Joy." I can still remember when I first realized the joy in *true* ideas. It is at that moment that we touch God. The modern outlook is to assume that everything is based on our own likes, dislikes, preferences and that there is no absolute. But God created a world based on truth. Spirit is more true and more real than anything of the physical world. There is nothing without spirit. And nothing is more exciting than those moments when we touch spirit in some way, or grasp it, for a moment, in thought.

I am deeply saddened by your story because it is so common these days. How different this world would be if there was only more caring and nurturing of one another. The worst criminals of all are those with the power to make changes who, instead, preserve the selfish, greedy control of wealth and pretend the homeless and needy do not exist. The attention is so much on the physical. Scientists think we live in the most enlightened times. They are wrong. We live in the darkest of times, when our consciousness of spirit is dead. Yet it exists and can be found, not only in ourselves, but in everything and in everyone—even in your jailers.

Your attitude that you feel you've been rescued is a great way to look at it, and I'm sure it's true. You asked about there being a positive and negative in every occurrence. I haven't thought about it in that way, but perhaps so. I've thought, rather, that every event has a reason and that it always can be made into something positive.

I'm also impressed that you recognize that you've missed something. There is a wonderful lot we know nothing about, and it is a great experience to go in search of it—and wonderful that we have so many lives so that learning and growing never stops. It gives me great joy to be able to offer you what I can.

Did I tell you that I live in the country about four miles from town and have no visible neighbors even though my piece of land is only one and three-quarters acres? There are a few small animals, like squirrels and rabbits, who keep hidden most of the time, and lots of birds. In spring and fall, millions of birds go by on their travels north and south, making so much noise. I love it.

I am still thinking about your confrontation with the guards, and what you said about working very hard on your temper and stubbornness. You know, the best way to do this is not to try to control yourself or suppress it, but rather to try for a change of attitude, of mind, of understanding and try to work at Christ's way of compassion and love, even toward those who crucified him. Do not turn off your anger. You may have good reason for it. Do not let it get into your actions, let it stay in the realm of feeling.

There is a way I have used feeling in difficult situations. Mine had to do more with pain. I have had periods of intense pain. The natural reaction is to try to turn it off. One day I tried, instead, to experience it fully, to let myself be thoroughly immersed in pain, to feel it intensely. And it worked. The pain actually eased. It is useful with any emotion—jealousy, despair, anger. Emotions are very important and useful and should be cultivated. Then, oddly, they do not control us. If one meditates on each of the emotions, one learns, gradually, to see their true meaning. Let your feelings work during meditation.

I hope you were able to keep the sayings, meditations, and poems that I sent you, even if you were not allowed to keep the folder itself. But in the end I guess it doesn't really matter. The only permanent things in life are what you carry in your heart, what you become in your soul. That, one continues to have even after death.

I am looking for a book for you called *Love Can Open Prison Doors*. Your story reminded me of it. The author, Starr Daily, came near death in solitary confinement where he had an experience of Christ. Afterward, he learned to use love as a force for change. I've heard it said that love is the Eleventh Commandment given by Christ. Love is all-inclusive. A person who truly loves would probably not break any of the commandments. Does that make sense?

Love, hope, caring,
Ruth

———————

August 29, 1988

Dear Ruth,

I hope I don't have a funny way of looking at things, but until I came to confinement my spiritual awareness was practically zilch. There I met a spiritual aspirant, and I realized how undeveloped my spiritual self was. Now, I am trying to fill that void. I used to smoke cigarettes and marijuana alike. I had the idea instilled in my psyche that I could not quit without clinical help, and believe me, I have made attempts in the past and could not. After I started discovering my true self and needs, I dropped those habits like hot potatoes. It's amazing how people go through many changes looking for happiness and contentment and the answer to all of this lies in the truth.

I am thinking that it must be wonderful to be on your one and three-quarters acres away from the obstacles and other nonsense that exist in the city and urban areas of our society. It seems to me the less noise and traffic I'm around, the more tranquil I am.

Love yah!
Martin

———————

September 2, 1988

My dear Martin,

How right you are that only truth can set us free. Unfortunately, it is not yet a very popular notion.

An article has come to me about street kids. It is unspeakably horrible that a government like ours allows such conditions. We all must take responsibility for the conditions we allow to continue. It is poison. Not only are there poisons physically in the water, food, and air, but in thinking and feeling. I always come back to how it starts with each of us changing that part of the world which is ourselves. You can be sure that no matter where you are, as you learn and grow and change your thinking and feeling and your habits and behavior, it has a real effect in the world.

Yes, it is good to live in the country, in nature. But I am like a hermit here, and that is the other side. The man from whom I bought this place wrote to me afterward, "It is a cultural wasteland." It has been so for me, too, with not as many cultural activities as I was used to in California—almost no concerts, art shows, theatre, and so on, except in larger cities far from the area where I settled. But it has been a place of spiritual training, and certainly a lovely place to be during such schooling.

With love and caring,
Ruth

———

September 11, 1988

My dear Martin,

I did find *Love Can Open Prison Doors* in a most interesting way. I wrote to a couple of friends who live in large cities and asked them to search for it in the libraries and used book shops. One called and said, "Ruth, you gave that book to me a long time ago." So she sent it, and I have just made several copies. I'll send you one. If you look on page twelve, I think, you will find his statement that the loving person becomes love. So that is an answer to your own, like experience.

I don't know how to explain why your dreams are clearer when you meditate before going to sleep, except that in sleep we are in the spirit world—the same place as between death and a new birth. For you, the meditation seems to bring that world more to consciousness, which is what the study of "spiritual science" is about. Dreams are usually in the form of symbols and are difficult to interpret. Dream books are no help at all. So, I highly recommend continuing the practice of meditating on it before going to sleep.

You asked if love can sin. People try to fit the idea of sin into a rigid place of black and white. I guess there is such a thing as sin, but nothing like the way most people think of it. In the school of life, we are given lessons and testings and the possibility of improving. Things are not so fixed, and I also feel that the angels are growing and learning as well. If, when we learn to tell the difference between what is good and what is harmful, and if we then consciously, deliberately, choose what is harmful, we can probably call it sin. In that case, love could not sin for it would not choose to do harm.

So, till next time, love,
Ruth

———————

September 15, 1988
Dear, dear Martin,

It might be a good idea to discuss the subject of anger. There is nothing in your letters that gives any indication of anger, yet your incident with the guards must have had anger in it. Anger is one of the most difficult things to eradicate from oneself, among the last to hang on when one is working on overcoming unwanted elements in ourselves. Once I did some meditation on it. I tried to deeply experience anger and come to an understanding of it. Oddly, what I discovered was that it takes hold of one as if it has a life of its own. Like alcohol or drugs take over, and one's own individuality is no longer in charge, so does that happen with anger. And it grows deep, deep roots that are difficult, terribly difficult, to eradicate. Trying to turn it off is almost impossible. It has to be replaced with other things with which one can gradually fill oneself, like peace and love. And it should be done as an exercise during times of quiet and meditation, because once anger has been stirred, one is hardly in charge. Did I send you the peace poem/meditation, which speaks of love not as something passive, but as a force and a power? It should be thought of as such.

Fall is here. Light breezes keep the leaves moving outside my window. The house is surrounded by trees, mostly oaks. It is amazing how loud acorns sound falling on the roof. Each fall I continually start to go to the door to see if someone is there, until I get used to it. There are branches falling, too. I'm no longer able to pick them up from the yard, and it begins to look a bit shaggy. However, I kind of like the shaggy look. I am a peasant at heart and feel a kind of hominess with it.

A session at the dentist on Monday has left my mouth sore even after three days. But it's not too surprising—two badly infected molars had to be pulled. The worst is over. I generally heal quickly. My body seems to be getting older—well it does, of course, but one suddenly feels it. Walking is more difficult, and I find myself using the wheelchair a bit more. I have a terribly difficult time getting used to not being active and independent. I was *so* active and able to do so many things, even repairs. Now I have to get someone to change a light bulb.

Love,
Ruth

———————

September 19, 1988

My dear Ruth,

You are right when you say that most of these guys in here are very lonely. Most of us not only lose contact with outside society, but our relatives as well. I think it's a very beautiful thing for you to take time out to write us the way you do. Also the literature you've sent me is an abundance of blessings.

If only I could put into words the feelings I get after reading your letters and maintain them, I would be like the sun, which shines on everything without partiality. You are frightfully wise, wonderful lady! I say this in reference to your statement concerning anger. You see you are right in your assumption that my anger was a major factor in contributing to the incident. Had I been more in control of myself rather than letting anger take control, I'm sure the situation would have been less explosive.

Sometimes after I get through reading some of the literature you send me, I am elated and bursting with happiness and excitement at these new discoveries; naturally, I want to share them with somebody, but there doesn't seem to be anybody around here that's interested. That doesn't dampen my spirits, though. I normally lie down and try to digest it all.

After reading about the loudness of the acorns, I started laughing because I know if I were you, I would have been looking for a ghost or something a long time ago.

I thank whatever forces that are responsible for bringing us together. If you ever have anything to say to steer me in the right direction, please take no regard for my sensibilities because my trust and love for you is without fault.

To Ruth with eternal love and caring,
Martin

———————

September 29, 1988

Dear, dear Martin,

Your letter stirred me deeply and even brought a few tears. People with true sensitivity and the ability and the wish to search for deeper reality are very rare, indeed. It is not surprising that you do not find anyone with whom to share your new discoveries. It is hard enough to find such people outside of prison.

A friend from California came to visit. We have seen each other rarely over the years, but a great closeness exists between us. She wants me to stay with her in California, at least for the winter, or as permanently as life will allow. It is an urging that I can't refuse. I've been wanting to leave here for about five years but am tied to a house that doesn't sell. One needs lots of money in California, but there is always the possibility of magic and this may give me an opportunity to find out. So, unexpectedly, I'm on the way "home." I lived there for about thirty years, and it is the only place in the world where I have truly felt at home. It is in the middle of California, on the coast, and is exceptionally beautiful, with a great combination of ocean, mountain, and forest. I hope you may have a chance to see it one day. Well, the dear angels are helping, I'm sure, for suddenly there is someone to look after my house and car.

I wonder if it would be helpful to try to understand the feelings of the guards, of their very difficult job and their fears and frustrations. Don't expect much in the way of wisdom or understanding from people. Just try to develop it in yourself no matter what comes to you from others. That is a lot to ask, but oh, so worthwhile and oh, so difficult! Every time one fails it is necessary to be ever so patient with oneself and simply keep trying.

It is important not to expect visible results as we do inner work. The effort is what is important and to keep making efforts. Results come when the spirit world finds us ready. One works for transformation. It does not happen by fighting what is there now, but by concentrating on what one wants to develop. By cultivating love and understanding, one gradually becomes loving and understanding. Try to experience what motivates people. Do not necessarily speak to them about it, but experience it in your own heart. As you experience things, watchfully, what at first is just "probings" will become real for you. In time what is right will become more evident. You can expect there will always be questions and unsureness and new things to learn. That is the process of growth, of evolution—worldly and individually. Take joy in the process itself, as you are evidently doing now. The world you are learning about has always been there, but until one begins to "see" and "hear" it, until one says *yes* to it, it remains invisible. Then one begins to tread an actual path, which is the same for all students, with individual circumstances for each, as needed. If one is watchful, it begins to be evident that one is also guided by angels and guides who watch over us. We are also helped and watched over by the dead with whom we are connected.

These are thoughts that came with waking early this morning while thinking about you. It is good to watch what comes on waking. It is good to think about questions just before going to sleep, or about people or things, one wants to understand.

Your description of "being like the sun and shining on everyone and everything without partiality" is beautiful. It is a Christly experience. It is a picture of what to strive for. It is love, expressing.

With love,
Ruth

October 6, 1988

Dear Martin,

I'm finding it hard to sleep these nights. I've been thinking of the trip, gathering things, wanting to project my mind into the things I will need in California for a stay of several months. Little gets done because I move so slowly. My legs are very uncooperative and exhaustion is a constant companion, but that is not new. I have been tired for a very long time. But I know all is well, although the mortal part still gets anxious, and this is fine, too.

Last night when I lay down to sleep, I thought about what it will feel like to be back in the area I love and to go back to my old haunts—the shore, rocks, sea otters, sea gulls, and all the other familiar things. In Pacific Grove, one can drive the car right down close to where the otters live, and I can walk to the water using a cane, sit on the rocks, watch the waves come up and down along the shore, see and hear the birds, and smell the ocean. I imagine which streets I'll choose to go to the shore, and what the fog will feel like. I did not expect to ever get back, and until my friend appeared here with her magic wand, it was the last thing on my mind.

I hope you will come here someday and see how very beautiful it is. I picture the door of your cell opening and freeing you from your confinement, and then the door of the prison letting you free. And I hope for you a new, a different life. It will not be easy to find your way. The world does not help. Do not try to be of the world. Find your own inner being. That is true freedom. Be in the world, but not of the world. The world is not loving. Be loving. The world does not want truth. Be truthful. The world does not want true knowledge. Make it your quest.

All this has to be learned, and it has to be practiced quietly, secretly, while you pretend to be like the others. They think that pleasure consists of gadding about, drinking, carousing, watching ball games, punching one another in boxing rings. They are wrong. The greatest pleasure is in discovering ideas, opening doors to spiritual awareness, walking in nature—in the woods and mountains, along the ocean, communing with the animals and birds, in feeling/hearing nature sing and in singing along with it. Joy is exchanging great ideas with people, asking questions of one another, making each other think. It was good to have that with Ellen here—the first time in oh, so very long. When I started reminiscing, I remembered a few cards among my stationery from long ago, so here is one—an ocean scene. It is amazing that I shall see it again.

I like to think that real freedom will come for you soon, first inside yourself—like the poem, "not from outside in, but only inside out." The outside will come, too. What you do inside will eventually change the outside. Be patient. Don't let setbacks or difficulties worry you. It is the natural process. For selfish reasons, I want the process to happen quickly so that we may have an opportunity to meet. But in any case, whether in this world or the next, real friendships continue on.

I have not told you much about myself. I have an old body that is hard to get used to when one has always been very active, and when the spirit is still young—a tired, old uncooperative body. There is some arthritis, a bad spine, but luckily very little pain, just the kind of achiness that old people get. One can live with that. Each of us has our own kind of confinement. But age brings, also, its own kind of gifts. I am blessed in many ways.

It is a good thing to know that there is an individual inside yourself that can be found, and that you don't need to imitate the world. And you can create and mold that inner self and make it anything you want to be. It is good to realize that help is there for the very hard struggle necessary to make that shaping possible. In whatever direction you decide to go, whatever road you choose, all your effort will be rewarded. Do not look for reward. That comes invisibly, of itself, when you are not looking, in ways you can never imagine. Keep on trying, not giving up. There is no real arrival point, for the road goes always to new places. There is always a further goal, beyond where one is at any time. Then one learns the joy in the doing, itself, and in every little gain and asks no more from life than that it continue so.

I carry you in my heart and mind,
Ruth

October 10, 1988

My dear Ruth,

I have just finished reading your letter once again. Your words and love move me and touch things within me that have been lying dormant. Truly I am discovering the real me with each new day and a great thanks is owed to you. Thank you, dear Ruth!

Your letter, and especially the prayers, brought tears from me also. I have never experienced anything like it. If this kind of stuff had been given to me in my ignorance, I would have scorned the giver, but now that I am being given life, there is no greater treasure in the world and may God bless the giver.

I am glad to hear about your good fortune concerning California. Your excitement and anticipation are contagious because I feel as though I'm going with you. Therefore, our happiness is one. Sometimes when I'm thinking about nothing in particular, all of a sudden I start smiling with joy and happiness because I am thinking of you.

Lovingly,
Martin

CHAPTER 2

Finding Love

October 17, 1988

Dear Ruth,

Oh, Ruth! If you only knew how dear you have become to me. You have helped transform my life from the dead to the living. You have succeeded where all else has failed—the law, family advice, legal counseling, and everything you could think of. Sometimes I stand at the back of my cell looking over the horizon in the evening when the sun is going down, a beautiful sight to behold, and I take a real good look at myself—my spiritual self—and I laugh with joy. Whenever I smile now, it's a joyful smile, and then I think of you dear lady, and I cry with joy because I am so full of joy. I have never known that life can be so beautiful.

Ruth, I feel, when one finds freedom from within, it is just like beauty, peace, and love. One finds these qualities in all things, even this cell. Some of my fellow prisoners are telling me I'm starting to act kind of strange. I don't see it because I try to stay in tune with this environment also. But I've been thinking that everybody else is changing for the better.

I do hope you will enjoy your trip to California. Though I'll not be there in the flesh, I will definitely be there in spirit and love. In my mind I pictured the scene you described in your letter, and I will definitely try and get there one day.

To Ruth from Martin, with love!

October 21, 1988

My very dear Martin,

It is very gratifying to see the signs of real progress in your letter. Perhaps there is also need for a little caution, a sober outlook at what will be a difficult struggle. Progress does not happen in a straight line. There are ups and downs—times when we are given very difficult exercises/training. You are on the start of a "path" that is difficult and wonderful. Opening one's eyes means seeing ever more, the beautiful and the ugly, and facing them all with equanimity.

You will need to know, too, that it is a lonely experience, and you will not be able to share it with many. The ones who are closest to you may be just the ones who will not understand. They will know that you are different, yet not understand what it is. At the same time, it is necessary to be realistic and know that it may not be liked. Being different seems to antagonize a great many people. Some of the greatest and gentlest beings on earth have been crucified and assassinated. Think of Christ, Lincoln, Gandhi, Martin Luther King, Jr., and many others. In subtle ways a good many people feel threatened by goodness, gentleness. It is important to know and to understand this. Be aware of how people will choose destruction and fear and hate. No matter what one's background or rationalization, it is, ultimately, a choice. When the "light" goes on, it is because the person, himself, has chosen it. It is, in one way and another, offered to all. Usually, one has to hit bottom, and this is individual for each person.

I am including my Carmel address. The friend I'll be staying with is Japanese. I just learned she was born in our own form of a concentration camp when we interned the Japanese during the war.

Love always,
Ruth

October 27, 1988

Dear Martin,

You asked about vegetarianism. I have found it to be better for my health. But just as important, is that it be unadulterated, unsprayed, without additives. In other words, natural. When God created the world, he knew what he was doing. (Funny that we have to be reminded of this.) It was meant to be a whole (how else could it be) just as it was designed. We can't improve it, only destroy the fine balance. If we continue as we are going, we could make it uninhabitable. Let us hope there is an awakening before that. People are starting to think about it, and that is the beginning.

It is also important to realize that thinking in itself is an active force. Even now, when you are unable to be active in the world while being locked up, the kind of thinking you do makes a difference.

We all have spiritual guides, in the physical world, in the spiritual world. We are given opportunities to develop, step-by-step. There are obstacles and pitfalls along the way. Like any schooling, the lessons become more difficult. But as we learn, there is also greater gratification—excitement in new discoveries, and even in the struggle. And sometimes we have moments of real enlightenment and a sense of being at one with reality. Perhaps you experience that.

One thing that can help us to deal with some of the harshness is to become aware of the long expanse of time, knowing we have been here from the beginning of earth's evolution, that we evolve with it, that we shall continue on with it for a time of which we can have no concept. It gives one quite a different relationship to the present moment, not that it is less important, but more, because we have an effect on the whole future of the earth. On the other hand, the kind of materialistic thinking we do in present times becomes less important, the thinking that sees the present as all there is so that people try to grasp the superficial as all important. That young people are committing suicide in such great numbers now, even in groups, is a sign of the emptiness they experience. They are given no substance. But you know that!

People use so much alcohol these days. It is important that we become more conscious, more aware, not dreamy. Alcohol fights that, dulling the consciousness. It also, supposedly, stays in the body for quite a long time even after one stops drinking. Alcohol, as do drugs, also attracts very negative elements from the spiritual world and this can be sensed in bars and places where drinking goes on. It could account for some of the weird and horrible crimes that take place. When a person is not in charge of his own being, that leaves an opening for it to be possessed. Later on the person has no recollection of what took place; actually, he was not really there. I'm sure there are prisoners who have had this happen.

The trees are beautiful now, all dressed in their fall colors.

Love always,
Ruth

———

November 8, 1988

Dearest Ruth,

Here is a picture of me and my three sisters that was taken in 1981. My features aren't too clear because it was taken at night outside a bar, and as you can see, I am of a dark complexion. I have seven sisters and these are the three oldest. I haven't really changed except I've gotten more muscular, fifteen or twenty more pounds.

Ruth, I doubt very seriously if what I have found can be put into words, but I do know that I have a much longer way to go and I do want to go much farther. There are times when I am just lounging around, thinking of nothing in particular, and I get insights into certain things and a beautiful quiet calm enfolds me; I feel as though I am one with all things. I think this is one of the most beautiful feelings a person can ever experience. I am always thinking of you.

I am learning that words are not sufficient to express our deepest and most inner thoughts, and I am realizing newer and better ways to express myself in ways that words can never do. As you so eloquently stated, I am also beginning to view life as a classroom. When I start viewing things more objectively, the better am I able to see things more clearly. Isn't it amazing what bias and prejudgment can do to hinder our acute senses and spiritual growth!

You know, I find it very interesting how much easier it is to get around or deal with adverse situations once a person exercises patience and understanding toward their fellow humans. I have taken to practicing these two qualities with my fellow prisoners and guards. The effects are so astounding that I am compelled to continue this new and beautiful experience.

Love yah!
Martin

———————

November 13, 1988

Dear Martin,

I arrived here three days ago and was picked up at the airport by Ellen and Tom. They welcomed me like family. Today my friend Diane drove me along the ocean for my first view of it. The ocean is still there, the waves washing up on shore, and the long stretch of white sand for which Carmel is famous. Then we went to her house for a home-cooked fish dinner. We were such good friends, and it was like a continuation of the past—enthusiastic, bubbly, philosophical, joyous, catching up on the time apart. We met many years ago in a small school in Monterey. She was the kindergarten teacher, and I was the school secretary. We loved one another at once and had good times together. It was a different world then, and we have watched so much go down hill—the drug era come in, the lessening of integrity and honesty, and so on. Yet, in more invisible ways, people do progress, grow more sensitive, are kind and dear, and that is growing, too, but not so much where it can be seen outwardly.

It is impossible, without writing books, to describe this place—its culture, its way of life, the beauty of nature. I am an outsider after so much time away, yet it is home, the only place I have ever felt at home on earth.

Your picture arrived and I am so glad to have it. I assume you will want it back after I have lived with it for a while.

I wonder if I ever told you about my background? I am a first generation American of Jewish parents who came from Russia. My parents were atheists, and we three children were brought up to be atheists as well. I was thirty before I realized that was not right. The good thing is that it left me free to think about it on my own—to find my own way into the world of spirit. They were fine people, with goodness and love, and we had a good childhood. They were also very unprejudiced; we had a black couple among our close friends.

I think of you in confinement, and I suppose it has some good points as well as bad. I think of all the time you have for study and meditation.

I love you, too. Keep writing.
Ruth

―――――――

November 24, 1988

My dearest Ruth,

I give praise and thanks to the infinite creator who is responsible for bringing you into my life and making it a brighter world in which I live. I am ecstatic to hear that you have received the picture at last. It is yours to keep for always— your happiness is my happiness, of course. I am praying that you will be living in California by the time I'm released from here. You have a beautiful way of describing people that makes me love them instantly, and I now feel that Diane is part of our family.

As for confinement, if I view this cell as such, then this is all it ever will be. My present philosophy is to look for high things in lowly places and lowly things in high places.

Love yah!
Martin

―――――――

November 26, 1988

Dear, dear Martin,

I sent a postcard this morning with the face of a sea otter. Isn't he beautiful?

I love your picture, and the smile, which is almost all I can see from where the picture is on the shelf near my bed. I hope that when you have an opportunity you will get a current picture for me.

It is wonderful and magical to be here. A friend took me for a walk along a trail near the ocean. I sat on a bench while she walked and watched and listened to the ocean. You know, in all my vivid memories of the ocean, I did not remember how very loud it is. The waves were strong, moving with serious determination, bringing in the tide. The next day we went again. The waves were a bit more quiet, joyous, gay, but every now and then there came a large, roaring one, just enjoying its own movement and thundering sound. Someday when you come to see my favorite place on earth, if I am not here, you can think of me and speak to the ocean and listen to its moods. And I will hear you both from wherever I am.

My friend lives in Berkeley, near San Francisco. She has been as lonely in this metropolis as I have been in Missouri. The "path" is a lonely walk. At the end is a different kind of union, with all life. But one goes alone, just as birth, death, pain—all the various hungers—are one-man deals. I know you are dealing with much of this in your present experience. It is for growth. Sometimes I feel it with you, for we each have our own form of prison experience and therefore can understand and feel compassion. I hope you can be frank and do not feel you always have to "put on a happy face" for me. Without frankness, without the opportunity to say, "I hurt," what sort of a friendship is it? And aren't we family—spiritual family, which is the deepest of all?

Lóve, dear Martin,
Ruth

———

December 1, 1988

My dear Martin,

Yesterday I saw a copy of *Winnie the Pooh* in a store, and I wanted to buy it for you. But then I thought, "Who at your age has not already read *Winnie the Pooh*? But, I know some have not, for I was about thirty-seven when I first heard my second husband read it to his two children. And I loved it. Then, I thought of *The Little Prince* and the *Narnia* tales. Let me know about all three. They are children's books for all ages, filled with whimsy and wisdom. If children were brought up on such books, we would have less prisoners. I consider books a necessity, so one by one, as you will be permitted to have them, I will continue to send what I can. My mother was very wise in these matters. During very poor times, and in the depression, she somehow managed to find the means to continue our music lessons and to make sure we had access to books through the libraries. Cultural things were considered by her to be absolute necessities, along with food. She was right.

We like to look upon these times as enlightened, but ignorance and darkness are rampant in the world. People think the most important thing is to develop clever mechanical devices, but spiritually these are the darkest times. And improvement will not come from those in power. For the most part, they only think in terms of perpetuating that power. Only as each human being takes his own development in hand, each working on himself, will there be a change. So it is up to you. As you change yourself, so do you change the world. Each of us is given an individual body and soul and mind—some of the talents spoken of in the Bible—which we must learn to increase, and that increase is given back to the world. One must be careful not to grow self-important in the process and to keep a certain humility. Our good angels are with us and they let us know when we stray.

Love always. I keep you in my heart and mind and prayers.
Ruth

———

December 5, 1988
Dearest Ruth,

As I sit here and begin to write this letter, my mind is bubbling with thoughts and energy. There are so many things I want to say, so many endearments I want to express. But I know no words to express what I truly feel. Perhaps the simplest thing to say is, "I love you!"

Yes, they do have an educational program here, but it is not for inmates on close management. However, we can get correspondence courses on our own. I have had plenty of opportunities over the years I have been incarcerated, but I've always been too busy getting into mischief and rebelling. Yes, I have an interest in getting an education and I realize there always was, but I kept it suppressed because of my rebellious nature. Little did I realize how much I was denying myself all the enlightening benefits and wonders that stem from education. I am writing to the address you sent me of the state library to see what kind of correspondence courses are available.

Coming to Carmel will be like a pilgrimage for me whenever I am released from prison. Sometimes I envision myself going by the shore, and I try to capture the same beautiful serenity that only the soul can hear, that you describe in your letters.

The guys here are not inclined the same way I am, but I guess each of us in our own way is constantly seeking. The most common discussion is about homosexuality, which often leads to violence. Some who are educationally inclined like to have literary debates, quoting Plato, Socrates, Confucius, and other great philosophers; this generally leads to hostility. The religious guys often end up hating each other because of their different views concerning God. Sometimes I am called on to settle their disputes and I begin to feel a sense of pride until I realize that people who can be provoked into harming each other over such trivial matters can't be too smart. That dispels my false pride. Afterward I sit down, like I am doing now, and write letters to loved ones. Whenever I do that, I like to write about love, peace, happiness, and so on. In order for me to do that convincingly, I have to be able to feel it myself. So, if it seems to you that I am happy in all of my letters to you, Ruth dear, it's because I am. Each time I sit down and write to you I always read over your most recent letter and try to recapture the beautiful feelings I get when first reading them, and it always works. These are the wonderful and heavenly things that you inspire within me. This prison is a place laced with mostly violence and hostility, but if one can silence the false impression of things and see them as they really are, one can find beauty anywhere, even in prison.

Love always,
Martin

December 5, 1988

Dear, dear Martin,

Diane took me to a Christmas concert, and I brought your letter along to share with her. You must meet her when you come, even if I am not here, and I have asked her to introduce you to my favorite music, that of Bach, Mozart, Handel, Telemann, and so on, their chamber music.

Did you get the otter cards? What wonderful faces they have! Of course, one cannot see that from the shore, so the cards are especially precious. And there is a picture of two seals. Mrs. Seal on the left is smilingly reminding you that joy is worth cultivating, and on the right, Mr. Seal is saying, more seriously, that it's a good world, but much depends on how we make it. Make it good for yourself and others. We make the world better by making our small piece of it better. That is what God wants of us, and Gandhi is all for it, too, as he will tell you, himself, in his own biography. Would you believe, after all this time, the Gandhi is on my table here ready to mail and in time to be your Christmas present from me.

One way to become educated is by reading a lot, even if you are unable to get a correspondence course. It need not be any special course, just good literature.

When we have a chance to meet you will find me quite human, with a goodly share of faults and stupidities. When we have overcome our faults, we will become angels and no longer human beings. Faults give us something to strive for and teach us humility and are some of the gifts given us by God. So do not expect too much.

Much love, dear friend,
Ruth

———

December 10, 1988

Dearest Ruth,

I have never read *Winnie the Pooh*, the Narnia tales, or *The Little Prince*, but since they are highly recommended by you, I'm sure I would like to read them. Because you say they are for children, I am more eager to get them than ever. In many ways, kids are the most blessed among the living. They are commonly without guile, prejudice, pretense, and so on. I remember when I was a child, I was in love with everything and everybody. It was only when I started growing up in the world that I learned not to love so easily and so freely. I can better understand now what Jesus meant when he spoke about "becoming as little children."

The methods used in *Love Can Open Prison Doors*, for using love, work wonderfully. Yet, when confronted with certain negative forces, I stay away from the people until I can better master myself. I'm getting better with time, but must still be on guard against myself. The great master said, "Marvel not that you have control over the spirits because to whom much is given much is required."

Oh, yeah, the Gandhi autobiography has arrived and I'm in love with it already. How can I ever repay you? Oh, I know. I must do that which is required. (Smile) Christmas began for me after I received your first letter, and it's getting better with time.

Love,
Martin

———

December 20, 1988

My very dear Martin,

You have given me the best Christmas present of all, and it is that you want to continue your education.

You are making a really good start in staying away from the negative forces. It takes time to learn to send love against it rather than respond in kind. There are many times, as I read your letters, that I want to hug you. Feel yourself being hugged.

As for a means of paying back, one friend taught me years ago that one does not necessarily pay back the person who has helped you, but passes it on to another. Life gives us plenty of opportunity for that.

When trying to learn to love people who were difficult for me to love, I would think of them during quiet moments and picture them created by God. I tried to see the spirit being, which gets hidden by a lot of "gook." We all have a long way to go, lifetimes. We are in process of "becoming," not fixed in our present state. We don't know why a person behaves in a certain way, at a certain time, what lessons are being learned, what training for future work. The direction we are going, the inner work, does get better with time, but not easier. Like any training, the lessons must get more difficult as we grow. But then the difficult things give us more joy and a sense of accomplishment. And doing what is good and right—though it can be hard to recognize—has its own compensation, built in.

I send you much love. God be with you, dear friend,
Ruth

————————

December 26, 1988

My dear Martin,

Thanks for the so beautiful Christmas card. It is the nicest one I have received, and I do love it very, very much.

I am staying at Diane's house for a few days. She cooked a beautiful Christmas dinner of goose and all the things to go with it. I gave up being a vegetarian for the evening and thanked the bird for giving us nourishment as well as good taste. We listened to good music and talked. Then I got out your letters, and since you had given me permission to share them, we read them aloud together, first she reading and then I. I think she will not mind that I tell you she cried at times, as I, too, sometimes do when reading them. It was a new experience, hearing them like this from someone else, and I found new things I had not quite heard, or possibly not remembered, before.

Tomorrow we will drive down the coast to visit a prisoner I have been corresponding with for several months. He has told me that there are thousands of men there, and I think, "What must the atmosphere be like in a place like that, with so much emotional stress in one place—so much heartbreak, frustration, pain, anger, violence, loneliness?" I am thinking how, in just such a place, you are changing and that the sensitive, loving being inside you is coming forth.

Yes, and you will find, as you change, that the world around you will change. Real freedom is when we are inwardly free. That comes only from hard work and from not being afraid of pain. So keep up your good efforts, dear friend. You will find it is easier to put aside hate and anger when we can see purpose in our lives. And it is part of the lessons that life brings—to remain humble, to know we are part of the problem, that we share the guilt, that the effort is filled with our own stumbling, bumbling clumsiness, but that we must keep trying. We are the problem and the answer, and most of us have little to be proud of.

What makes us cry in your letters are the beautiful thoughts, the sensitivity, the desire for change and growth, the love that you express. My spirit will always be with you, even when the physical body is not. I will delight in your struggles to make things better and will be there in your pain and feel joy with you at accomplishments, small and large.

We feel your presence, as I am sure you feel ours, and we send you love.

Blessings,
Ruth

———————

December 27, 1988

My dearest Ruth,

I have just read your letter and card again for the fourth time since receiving them. Your letter is heartwarming and filled with love and inspiration as always. But the card is, oh, so beautiful! And the poem, wow!!! Truly you are enjoying a beautiful kingdom of peace, love, tranquility. I want you to know that this beautiful card has given me more joy and peace than any material thing ever could for Christmas. Thank you so very much.

I send you loving good wishes for the coming year.

It is eleven o'clock at night and the lights in my cell have just gone out, so I'll leave you with my love until next time. Please feel yourself being hugged.

Martin

———————

January 1, 1989

Dear Martin,

Happy New Year, dear one, and so many good, good wishes!

Life is so full of mysteries. I think of the many prisoners there were in the visiting room where I saw my prisoner friend, most of them so young, and how "normal" they look, and how impossible it is to see, looking at them, that they had committed a crime.

The atmosphere of the prison was rather disturbing to me. It seemed that there was so much pain, concentrated. I felt it even at the highway before we entered the premises. So, I was in a strange state when we met, very quiet. He did most of the talking, and I learned a lot about him that he could not put into his letters. The visiting room is actually quite pleasant and relaxed and the guards, also, though they have a no-nonsense look about them. One could get food and drinks from coin machines in the very large room where there were comfortable seats and coffee tables, and there was a patio where one could walk outdoors when it wasn't raining. It appeared to be a very minimum security prison. The prisoners have keys to their own cells, and each one had his key hanging from his belt. If there is another opportunity, I may go back. I'll be more prepared for it then. I kept feeling, "So much pain!"

You wondered if growth toward God has an end. Probably not. In any case, we certainly have a long way to go. That things come to us at the right time, when needed, or when we are ready, is one of the wonderful things in life. I think of it as the work of the angels. Life can be more peaceful when we know the angels are there, always helping, bringing us the right people, books, and so on, just what we need. But we have to be receptive, cooperative, and "leave the door open for their gifts."

We must keep trying for your education.

Love always,
Ruth

January 4, 1989

My very dear friend, Martin,

How difficult it is to get a really true picture of each other. I send you my best, most inspired thoughts, feelings, writings, and you imagine that is all there is. Lately there have been more aches than usual, sometimes pain. I cannot walk without leaning heavily on the cane. My wheelchair is here, but a nice thick rug makes it too hard to move and the cane is easier. I read your last letter again earlier today, and now again; how you imagine I must always be peaceful, tranquil. You speak of my enjoying a "majestic and beautiful kingdom of peace, love, tranquility." Yes, there are such moments. They are moments. You say you are "laughing at yourself (having been inspired by my letter and poem) for trying so hard to reject a lot of hurts, disappointments, sadness, and other things that life has been offering as lessons lately." I am thinking of how we never write of such things. I don't think it is planned that way. We just naturally want to send the best to one another.

Events have happened (of themselves, no one's fault) in such a way that certain frustrations have built up—by a handicapped body, by a lack of transportation, by a lack of something truly absorbing to do. And in the end, I spent some thought and feeling trying to experience what it must be like to be caged in a cell. We all have our prisons. It is not so bad for me. I am old and no longer have driving passions and desires. I am not locked up in a small room, and there are many things I can do to keep occupied. And I think of you, really without an outlet. I have spent a lot of time today thinking about you and about others in like circumstances. There is no way one can truly understand it without experiencing it.

My life has not been tranquil and peaceful. It has been filled with frustration and heartache, hard work, hurt and disappointment, and betrayal by people I trusted and cared for. There have been good things, too, a mixture of everything we can experience on earth. There also has been terrible pain and despair and hopelessness. I no longer experience these things. Life is more peaceful and easy these days. But it is just because of the difficulties and pain that I am able to write helpful things now.

All the people I have known, and know now, who are particularly sensitive and kind and loving, have had a good share of hardship. And it has been good to have a day of frustration, of a little pain, of being brought to remember what others are experiencing. I am too well off to truly feel it, but I try not to forget how it is for others. I think of the homeless, the hungry, and for a moment am made uncomfortable by realizing my own comfort.

I come, in my experiencing, to Christ and his extraordinary deed in coming to earth, and I feel how we must take up the teachings he gave us and of how we are only at the beginning. It is a long task ahead—lifetimes. And in the end it is exciting. The frustration leaves. What is left is the thrill of the growth that is possible, the love to learn about, the reaching out to others, the greatness yet to be expressed, the changes for good that are possible, the hope and goodness and beauty, the overcoming. We shall have our downs and ups and grow wiser and better with each trial. And some things that seem so important will grow trivial with time. The contact with my prisoner friends is good for me. The Gods are good and wise to have arranged it so. Thank you for being my friend.

I send you much love, dear Martin,
Ruth

January 7, 1989

My dear Ruth,

I have just received the beautiful pictures of you, and I am still looking at the one of you and the dog. It's a captivating and beautiful scene, and it makes me want to jump into the picture and hug you both. After reading your letter, there are so many things I want to say, so many thoughts going through my head at one time. I'm sitting here bubbling with joyous laughter and love, wishing I could reach out and hug you. The part about you and Diane reading my letters the way you did is very heartwarming and touching. This is a memory I will keep and cherish for always.

I think I forgot to tell you that my mother and two of my sisters came to visit me for Christmas. It was a beautiful reunion. It was the first time in seven years that I had seen any of my sisters. Because I am on close management confinement I'm only allowed a one-hour visit every thirty days. I think we must have spent the whole hour hugging and expressing our love for each other.

You speak of my confinement. It is possible that I could get out, but I'm not sure how I would react to the guards if I were threatened by them in any way again. You see, my dear Ruth, I keep remembering the expressions on their faces, the anger, the brutality without regard for another human's life. I also have to deal with the fact that once an inmate is physically victimized, by guards or inmates, and does not retaliate, he is then looked upon as something weak and treated as such by the guards and prisoners alike.

Sometimes when I am looking out of my window, I have a nice view of the trees and cows and other things, even the sun going down. A most beautiful sight to behold. And then a beautiful calm enfolds my body, and I feel at peace with everything. It's as though I have become one with all there is. My feelings toward being in confinement are this: There are times when I feel like I can't take another minute without losing my sanity, but these thoughts are quickly conquered for fear of it really happening. There are times when I feel I am making progress on getting out, and then there are times when I just don't care. The best feelings of all are when I leave everything in the hands of God because I know that he will never give me more than I can bear.

Love always,
Martin

CHAPTER 3

What Is a Friend?

January 18, 1989

My dear Martin,

I, too, feel myself overflowing with love when I think of you and look forward to a time when we might have a real embrace in person. Perhaps we already know each other from the past.

You are very kind to be so caring about my physical condition, but really it's not bad. Another of the lessons life offers. I am so appreciative about there being so little pain. I do not think of illness and pain as a burden, but rather as one of the gifts of a wise world order. It is how we are taught to be better human beings. Without pain how would we ever learn love and compassion? And we would never understand joy. Everything that is given to us on earth has meaning. One of the lessons of spiritual development is to take all things with equanimity. I warn you, I will be using that term a good deal.

If we look upon the world realistically, we can see the deceit and know it without disappointment and hurt. We can recognize it and not expect it to be what it is not. We can transform ourselves, patiently, and not expect unrealistic miracles even of ourselves. The person you spoke of, who lied and felt ashamed when he realized you knew, has learned something. That is the important thing. He did not do it because he meant to lie to you. He has learned to lie and that is how he functions. That he had a moment of awakening about the meaning of lies is great. It is a moment to feel good about him.

You asked about being a friend. It is being available, caring, helpful. We all need to learn that. Once one has learned to live in such a way, so that it becomes one's natural, everyday behavior, then, in a subtle way, one becomes an example to others. Many people have never seen honesty and goodness.

They do not know *how* to be a friend because they have never really had one.

A young person, who was quite a liar, came to live with me when she was fifteen. She was so expert at it that, even when you knew she was lying, you wanted to believe her. Instead of fighting with her about it, or trying to lecture her, I simply told her I would not lie to her or for her. Very soon afterward the telephone rang and she said, "If it's Don, tell him I'm not here." It was and I said, "She says she's not here." She was shocked because that kind of lie seems to be acceptable by almost everyone.

In time it became truly helpful to her because she knew she could rely on me. She knew if I said something, she could trust it. I was always available to her and always helpful. I allowed her to be herself, yet was tough as I felt it to be needed. When she was picked up by the police for taking something from a store, I simply took her home and said little. Luckily the police called me and the matter was dropped. She never did it again. She never would talk to me—a sadness of our times—and so I would have to guess what she was going through and talk to her with suggestions, exposing, gently, things I saw without lecturing or pressuring her to say anything to me. It was a difficult time for me because I wasn't always sure what I was doing either. But the point is that, in a way, it was mostly by example, especially about the lying, for she could see that honesty has a reason.

The man is wrong. Real freedom is total responsibility. He has it backward. It has nothing to do with doing as you please, but with being free of the conditioning we are taught. It has deep spiritual meaning, like saying that you can do your own thinking. It means you can learn spiritual laws and live by them without needing to be told. It is what happened to you when you gave up drugs and smoking.

Much love,
Ruth

January 19, 1989

My dearest Ruth,

I'm giving what you said about my new way of being, not being solely dependent upon anyone else, a lot of thought. I don't know exactly why, but reading that piece of advice started my thoughts reeling like a storm. I hope it's not because I am doing the exact thing you are warning me against. I'm going to meditate on this later and tell you about it in my next letter. Please bear with me!

You are right in your assumption that I would not be hurt by you saying no to some of the things I might ask for, but then I am one of those people who doesn't require much. I had an experience last week that I want to share with you. I had a lot of newspaper clippings and magazines, that I was saving, stacked up inside my cell. The guards came inside last week with a garbage can, and they threw them inside the can. I tried to explain to them that these clippings and magazines contain facts that I like to refer to sometimes during my study periods. After they intentionally ignored me, the first thought that came to me was anger, and all of a sudden something told me to quit acting childish because I should never value anything that can be taken away so easily. The lesson from that experience taught me never to value the valueless.

Before the guards left, I quickly got a grip on myself and helped them get rid of the clippings and magazines. They started apologizing for having to take my things and that made me feel kind of awkward and embarrassed and wanting to apologize to them for making them feel they had to apologize to me for doing their job. But I decided against it because too many of the other inmates were listening, and I didn't want to give them the wrong impression. So, while the guards were doing their apologizing, I just stared at them, not knowing what else to do. They must have thought I was cracking up or something because they left my cell in a hurry after giving me a strange look. I really didn't want to laugh at their predicament, but after they left, I tell yah I had plenty of fun laughing at the whole experience.

I think the reason my mind started reeling after reading your advice about my change not being dependent on a particular person was that I have had a lot of bad experiences from putting the wrong kind of faith in friends, and all of this was due to my lack of understanding. Now that the veil of ignorance is being removed from my eyes, I know that within everything and everybody there is a friend because God is omnipresent. It says in Psalm 139:8: "If I ascend up into heaven, Thou art there, if I make my bed in hell, behold, Thou art there." Isn't that a beautiful statement!!!

My dear Ruth, you have a beautifully inspiring way of compelling me to pour out my heart to you, but sometimes I have trouble finding the right words to express myself. Do you know that lately I am finding it harder and harder to relate to a lot of things that these guys talk about, and the ironic part of it is I know why. I am really changing so it's obvious to me now. Can you imagine suppressing most of your thoughts for fear of offending others? That's me most of the time in my present environment. A lot of these guys here often look for or take the slightest thing said as a challenge. They are constantly trying to prove that they are just as much or more of a man than the next guy with brutality rather than love, with ignorance instead of understanding.

Would you believe a guy threatened to kill me today because I heard him asking for some smoking tobacco, and since nobody that smoked would give him any, I went out of my way to buy a pack for him? When he asked how much he owed me, without thinking, I told him nothing. That's enough to get someone killed who's not wise to the ruses used in tricking the supposedly weaker guys into homosexuality. One of the major deceptions used is to help someone out financially. After a person is too far in debt to get out, some try to get out by killing, suicide, robbing others, and the ones that don't possess courage are forced into homosexuality. By our unwritten laws of survival, the guy who threatened me today was justified. He is a newcomer on this wing and doesn't really know me, and with the help of the rest of the guys, I explained to him that I am not harboring any deceptive ideas toward him and was only sympathizing with his cause. I also told him, if he really felt threatened by me, to give it back. His answer was, "Do you have a light?" What a relief!

But for the grace of God I would have welcomed a chance to beat this guy's face in and turned the situation into a tragedy instead of a beautiful learning experience. My dear Ruth, you are the most wonderful blessing one can beget from above.

Love to everyone, and don't forget yourself,
Martin

──────────

January 24, 1989

Dear, dear Martin,

Sorry my telling you not to be dependent put you into shock. Did I push the fledgling too soon out of the nest? I guess your wings are not fully grown and feathered. But children are made to grow up much too soon these days. I was thinking how you need to use your own judgment as much as possible. You are doing marvelously, and we are proud of you. Know, too, that it is all right to be wrong, to make mistakes. Each is a lesson we can profit from the next time. When one falls, like the child learning to walk, you just pick yourself up and go on trying. One of the things they teach children in schools is that they must never be wrong. Among other ways that it is done, it also comes out of the fact that they give grades. Each child needs to grow at the best possible pace for herself/himself without being compared to others.

A good teacher brings out the best that is in each child. In the Waldorf schools, where I taught crafts, the teacher gives a report twice a year. It is done thoughtfully, with much care, to encourage, support, and help the student to do the best he is capable of and to work with the parents in this. Study is made so interesting that the children do not want to miss school. I have seen children pretend to be well when they were ill in order to be able to go to school.

You should know that the things I say to you are not "etched in cement." Even I can be wrong, but I will never intentionally tell you anything misleading. Do you suppose God can ever be wrong? Sometimes I think something weird got into the works when He created people. I'm so glad you can laugh at funny life situations. Perhaps it will be through humor that you can get through to your fellow inmates.

I haven't yet gotten to the second-hand bookstores to look for study materials for you. My body tries to act eighty, but I tell it I'm only seventy-two and to quit making it hard for me to walk. Thank God for lack of pain, just legs that don't like weight put on them.

Here are some answers to questions from my prisoner friend that I thought might be good to share with you, so I am sending a letter that is written to both of you. It seemed like a good idea, especially since some of the ideas are things we have discussed as well:

To my friends,

I write about things that have come up in the course of my exchange with you both. I have tried to think them through and to come up with answers, such things as: Do things need to make sense? Is reincarnation and karma valid? Is freedom total irresponsibility? Do we need knowledge at all, and is there such a thing as truth?

Truth must, by its nature, make us look into ourselves, as well as at life and the world in general. It must be the joining of all things and their interplay with one another, of the understanding of all creation as a oneness, wholeness, instead of the separate bits and pieces of unconnected information that is the present mode of thinking.

Does it need to make sense? If it does not, then we put everything into a place of unreality; we negate all that we are, know, experience. Then nothing matters and there need be no morality. Anything goes. There is no responsibility, no debt when we do bad, no need to pay debts, no karma, no need to be honest, no need to answer to God for our behavior. There are, then, no spiritual laws and no need to obey laws, either of nature or of man. Poison the earth, take from it what we want for personal gain, steal, be entirely self-centered, have corrupt courts, murder, rape, hate, anger, dope, violence, child abuse— all the negative things now so prevalent.

Being truly religious implies a belief in a supreme being with whom anything does not go! It implies the idea that there is spiritual law, that there is good and bad, right and wrong. It is not enough to say that there is a God, who created us, who looks after us; we need to recognize that there are rules of behavior and proper respect, from us toward God, toward man—toward God's creation. There is truth and goodness, caring and love, not just the mouthing of such, but action to suit.

By taking up drugs and alcohol and by saying, "We cannot know truth," we support and aid the letting go of one's own control over what we shall be and do and believe. One says, in effect, "I am not responsible for my own being, my own 'self.' I do not care, and I am willing to go into a kind of oblivion and let what will happen to me come without using my own judgment or control. Anything goes. Desires, however they affect others, are to be followed. There are no rules and I am not accountable." Very prevalent these days is the expression, "Nobody knows, nobody can know."

We are all guilty. We share the guilt. We have forgotten truth and the true laws. When Christ said, "Let him who is innocent . . . " he spoke for us all. Criticism is not proper here, but understanding, sharing of the guilt and finding the way out through finding truth. Make the search for truth the most important element in life, finding spirit reality — the sense in it, the way everything in the world stems from spirit groundings — and how it interweaves, and letting nothing deter us from that search and from starting to live according to spiritual law as best we can, while we struggle for ever more insight. Only when we have insight do we also have freedom. And, then, we have a desire for responsibility and goodness, caring and love, because then we can do no other.

Ellen has invited me to stay with her indefinitely. So this is now my home. I must still return to Missouri and sell my house.

You are right that God is omnipresent, but you still need to protect yourself from those in whom God is well-hidden. Evil is a fact and has to be dealt with in the world, also ignorance and prejudice. And you will indeed need to suppress your thoughts and true being just as you once learned to do with love when you were a child. I like your quote from Psalm 139:8. Beautiful! But know that hell is hell and will treat you hellishly. I guess I don't need to tell you that in your present situation.

Sometimes people combine things in their unconscious that do not necessarily belong together. With the conquering of anger and violence, it may seem that one would be "soft." Not so. And we may need anger at times, but controlled. Should we have no anger at all? Should one fight in self-defense? Gandhi felt we should not. But what would have happened if the war was not fought against Hitler? It may be that love can conquer all, but what if we have not yet learned that kind of love?

My young nephew lived with me at one time. He was six. In school there was a bully who began to pick on him. He was a gentle soul for whom fighting was simply not his way. He began to not want to go to school, and after some sleuthing, I found out what was wrong. Without saying anything to him, I arranged for a friend to get him into boxing-type play when next he visited us, even getting a bit rough and getting him to punch back. My nephew didn't need to fight; his attitude changed and the molesting stopped.

Love to you,
Ruth

―――――

January 29, 1989
My dearest Ruth,

I have given the statement about freedom being total irresponsibility a lot of thought, and I can't find any logic in it either.

Sometimes I just sit back in my cell without saying anything and listen to what others are saying. Within all the threats, hostility, and violence being expressed, I can recognize the unspoken cry for help—the silent plea to be understood and their reluctance to say what they truly feel for fear of being misunderstood.

Diane reminds me very much of my grade school teacher. She had a strict and gentle way of teaching combined. I still remember the way she taught us how to enjoy our studies in and out of class and how we should encourage and assist our fellow students who were slower at learning than others. I'm sure if it wasn't for her I wouldn't know how to read as well as I do. She was my first- and second-grade teacher, and now that I think about it, I lost most of my will and motivation to learn after passing her classes. This kind of teacher is very rare and special.

I have read the book *Siddhartha*, which you sent me, and it has affected me like no other book. It makes life and all of its intricacies seem so simple until it has me wondering if it really is.

You know something? When I am really paying attention, I can even hear the guards' silent plea to be understood. A few of them go as far as doing things for us that put them in trouble. This is one of their ways of reaching out, sometimes, and it is quickly misunderstood and taken advantage of by those of us who are void of understanding. I'm trying to become more adept, patient, and understanding at recognizing and dealing with this type of situation. Experience has taught me that one of the loneliest feelings in the world is to make a silent plea for help and understanding and not be heard. This has been my plight most of my life until now, thanks to you. I still remember reading your first letter. It wasn't so much the words, but rather the beautiful feeling, the sense of our spiritual relationship, comfort and ease, that came over me after reading your letter. You are also right about freedom being total responsibility because all of a sudden I feel freer than I ever have before and yet more responsible for our brothers and sisters that haven't come as far as I have yet. Since meeting you, I am constantly reveling in my new-found freedom.

I have just reread your letter of January 24 and the paper addressed to me and your prisoner friend. As usual, you have succeeded in stirring up my already set thoughts. (Smile) There is so much beauty and wisdom in what you say and that makes me want to grasp it all with an equal amount of intellect and understanding. I am suddenly reminded of what *Siddhartha* expressed concerning our thought patterns, intellect, and our sense of understanding. The difference, he said, is our intellect understands words, concepts, logic, proof and argument. Understanding goes deeper. It is neither for nor against. Intelligence is said to be just on the surface. A mind can know thousands of things. It can become a living encyclopedia but not have any understanding.

This thing truth that you speak of in your letter addressed to us is the most interesting and potent of all subjects. My intellect asks what exactly is truth and if there is such a thing? My understanding says of course there is! Truth says to me, you can hear me in two ways. You can hear me with your intelligence and your intelligence can say yes. This truth sounds logical, this truth sounds illogical, or yes, I agree with this truth or disagree with it. Intelligence is quantitative and can be measured by I.Q. Understanding is intelligence moving in depth, it is quality in-depth and cannot be measured. It has been said that understanding is oneness with all there is; it is neither for nor against. Some of my most revealing and happiest moments are when I'm in my most understanding state.

Before you came along, I was entertaining some serious thoughts as far as revenge goes. At the same time there was something deep within me that wanted to forgive, but I just didn't know why or how. With your help and that of the angels, I was able to forgive them and understand why. I know now that I was just as much at fault as they were, and before I can forgive my human brothers, I must first learn to forgive myself. No understanding soul can be so callous in forgiving one child and not the other.

Are you familiar with the Theodore Bundy case? This is the guy who was going around the country killing college coeds at random. Until I became familiar with his case, I hadn't really given my views concerning the death penalty any thought. Now that I think about it, I think it's a necessary deterrent for other Ted Bundys that will take life at random without giving any thought to losing their own.

Love you very much,
Martin

February 1, 1989

Dear Martin, dear,

I am thinking about your question about whether it is more important to be a friend or to have a friend. I think I would give both top billing, equally. It is wonderful to be a friend but having a friend gives us a kind of nourishment, which we need as well. A lot of people, these days, are starved for friendship and love. One could also ask that question about love, and I would say it is very important to love and to be loved. Even the natural love of parents is now confused. It often doesn't work as it should, and children grow up feeling unloved and not knowing what it is or how to give it. I'm sure that must be true for the majority of prisoners.

Do not think you have to expose to others what you are inside. They will only try to destroy it, and in your present situation, maybe try to destroy you because they cannot yet bear to see individual, free expression. They can have no idea, no concept, of anything outside their present limited understanding. In your present studies and changing, you will be entering a very lonely place because your family will most likely, also, not understand, even if they recognize a change for the better and are glad for that. There are the rules of behavior in prison, as you said, and you will have to *seem* to abide by them.

So, again, bye for now, with heaps of love to you, who are so easy to love.

Ruth

———————

February 3, 1989

My dearest Ruth,

How can one express in-depth and profound love for another with mere words? What have you done to me with your magical wonders? Me, who's supposed to be so tough, so hardcore, cold and affected by nothing—you have turned me into marshmallow. Are you a genie who has come to rescue me from my delusional world of nothingness? What!! Do you deny this? Oh well, perhaps you do not realize the potency of your magic, which makes me love you even more if such a thing is possible. I am affected so much by your letters that I want to cry with joy, but since I'm not good at shedding tears, I must suffer this joy in silence. I give you a big hug.

The books by Steiner arrived last night, and they are treasures. I've been reading one all day; I couldn't seem to put it down. I'm cooped up in this cell all day, and still there doesn't seem to be enough hours in the day to do what I want to do. Isn't that crazy? And the card is beautiful beyond description. Blessed are those who can give without remembering and take without forgetting.

I'm glad with you for making your decision to stay in California. I hoped you would because you seem so happy, so much at home.

Please give the family my love and hellos. Good night my genie!

I send you my heart,
Martin

———————

February 6, 1989

My very dear Martin,

I knew about Theodore Bundy. It was prominent in the news for a time. I wonder if the death penalty is really a deterrent? They say the crime of murder is pretty much the same in states where they have the death penalty and where they do not. But here is something to think about: Is it all right for the state to take a life when it is against their own law. In other words, is it less criminal for them to do it than the other person? Also, what does it really mean spiritually to take a life at any time, including war?

I am also thinking about how so many crimes are committed by prison authorities for which they would be put behind bars if they were done outside of prison, and society finds that quite acceptable. Even murder! That's pretty sick and something we might expect in other countries, but not in America. Where's our thinking?

In answer to your question, I don't think Christ was referring to the ego as the tempter but to an actual being. Christ actually promoted the development of the individual. Instead of looking altogether to the old books for the "laws," he spoke of going directly to the Father. I think he meant for people to think and to penetrate to understanding, each for ourselves. This only can be done by becoming a real "self" and searching for truth individually. One can use the word ego to describe that "higher self" that is capable of doing that. Only in its negative, undeveloped state is it egotism.

Your letter gives me much to think about. I am sending you a meditative verse that might be helpful at this time. It is good to take something that one feels right about at the moment and memorize it and use it regularly every day. This has to be your choice, and I offer it only as a possibility. There are teachers who have the wisdom to offer just what a person needs at a particular time. I am not one of them, but I can make humble offerings that may fit a particular situation and let you choose. There are, of course, many things in the Bible that can be used in this way. I have felt a special relationship to The Lord's Prayer and the Twenty-Third Psalm and have used them so.

I'm impressed that you like the Steiner books because so many people find them difficult. Maybe it is easier when one has had less education. I am not joking. It is, in a way, like when I learned massage and did well because I had no obstacles through previous other training. The person who had the greatest difficulty was a woman who had already been using a different method for twenty years. It is possible for education to develop the head overly and block the way to direct connection with nature and spirit. I had one year of college before my father had a heart attack and I had to go to work. I worked in the clothing industry as a sewing machine operator. Good training for the soul, if not the mind. What a lot of different things I have done in this life!

I found these interesting quotes in a book called *Perspectives* by Paul Brunton, "The basis of a seeker's relationship to a master should not be one of complete servitude and intellectual paralysis, nor one of totalitarian prohibition from studying with other masters or in other schools. He should keep his freedom to grow and his independence to choose. . . . " And, "It is a grave misconception to regard the mystical progress as passing mostly through ecstacies and raptures. On the contrary, it passes just as much through broken hearts and bruised emotions, through painful sacrifices and melancholy renunciations."

Heaps of love always,
Ruth

February 9, 1989

Dearest Ruth,

I've just watched the sun set, and it turned fire red as it sat above the trees in the background—what a sight!!! I think all of this close observation of the sun, the animals in the pasture and the forest, is making me into a nature freak.

How wonderful it is to have the special kind of love that comes from special friends. I wish we could have that here instead of violence and hostility. I'm kind of afraid to reach out with that kind of love for fear of being smothered. So I shall continue to grow inwardly until I feel it's safe enough to reach out. You see, my dear Ruth, I realize that at my present stage I am very vulnerable to a lot of negative things that may come my way, and this is also the reason I depend on you, and others like you, for the right kind of help. I am practicing the exercise of love, as described in *Love Can Open Prison Doors*, on a couple of guys here, but they are already kind of close to me, so I guess they are more susceptible to it than anyone else might be.

There is a lot of confusion going on right now between the inmates in this wing, so I'm going to end this letter because it's getting hard for me to tune in with you. Whenever I write to you, I always feel as though we're right in front of each other.

Heaps of Love! (I like the way you say that.)
Martin

———

February 11, 1989

My dear Martin,

Diane took me to a thrift sale, and I found a wonderful little stuffed seal, a baby seal with such a dear face. I wish I could send it to you. Boy, now wouldn't that be something if the other inmates saw a stuffed animal in your cell! (I realize it would not be permitted.) She immediately said to call it Martin. So that is his name. I may shorten it to Marty, but it is still named after you. It cost fifty cents. And for ten cents there was a wonderful little red-haired doll about five inches tall, with a sweet expression, wearing overalls of blue denim. I am calling her Joy.

I gave up dolls at the age of eight, deciding I was too grown up for dolls, so this must be a sure sign that I have reached my second childhood. Marty is sitting on the TV in my room and Joy is nearby, leaning against a vase with one yellow rose that Tom and Ellen gave me this evening. Another vase holds five deep red roses. Ellen insisted I have them, too. They bought a good many, and they are all around the house.

The things you write about help me to understand many things. I have the impression you have a fear of love, and how understandable that is. The kind of love I speak about expects nothing back. It loves freely, just flowing out. No one need ever know. I think that is the love Starr Daily found. How right you are to protect the inner, gentle soul that can still be hurt. People can be very vulnerable to what comes at them from the world, not only in prison.

I, too, try to picture you when writing. If you ever get a chance to get a more current picture, I hope you will get one for me. But I'm indeed glad to have this one.

Did I tell you my answer to your question about friendship? To have no friend is to be always hungry, to not be a friend is to be unfulfilled. I think we need both.

I enjoyed your description of the sunset. We need lots more "nature freaks" in the world. A better way to put it is: The world needs all the nature freaks it can get.

To find a true idea, or to delight in a sunset, can be a very special experience of joy. And in experiencing it, one gives something to the world that is needed so very much. Nature gives so much, and in receiving what it gives, we give back to nature and to the world what it needs as well. In this, and in our exchange with the angels, we bring life rather than add to the destruction. Yes, by watching, with appreciation, the sunset from the window of your cell, you already make a contribution toward changing the atmosphere of the place where you live. It is a tiny, tiny speck of light in a dark place and not at all an easy task to keep it glowing. It is important to know that, just in this small way, one begins to create a counterforce against the violence and hostility you have around you there.

And now it is very late and I will say goodnight to you and Marty and Joy and five red roses and one yellow one. I hope you are all right. I think of you especially much these days and send protective prayers and lots of love.

Again, friend, heaps of love,
Ruth

———————

February 13, 1989

My dearest Ruth,

The part of your poem that says, "What I am, what I strive to be is up to me alone," reminds me of the other night when a guy asked me what did I think the prison officials here were going to do with me after my confinement. Without giving it a thought, I told him what the prison officials do is not what's really important, but rather what I do. I don't know if he really understood what I was trying to say because he looked at me kind of cross-eyed and kept silent. Explanations are sometimes more confusing, so after seeing his expression, I just let it rest.

Your question concerning the death penalty—is it right for the state to take a life when it is against their own law—what a question! I find you guilty, Ms. Sanders, of questioning things too deeply. (Smile) Seriously speaking, these are the kinds of questions that make us more conscientious about accusing others. Your question makes me think of the question Pontius Pilate asked Christ when he asked him what is truth and Jesus answered him not a word. To my way of thinking, I can only feel the right answer deep within me and do that which is required of the righteous at heart.

The way you explain things concerning Christ and his actually promoting the development of the individual instead of looking to the old law books, and of going straight to the father, makes things a lot more clear. Thank you. Your advice about giving myself plenty of time to know, investigate, and experience things for myself is beautiful advice. Sometimes I find myself too impatient to know certain things, and while I am busy at being impatient, I cannot see the answer that is right before my eyes.

About dreams, do you know I actually saw myself coming to prison again for bank robbery before I even thought about doing it? The way the crime happened was so crazy and unbelievable that I must tell you all about it one day. The job was so easy to do that I am still wondering after ten years what could have possibly gone wrong. It seems to me that I was destined to get caught, which reminds me of something I read about people being born and placed into situations whereby they may fulfill their karma.

To all the friends whose pictures you sent me to see, I shall now open the door to my heart and place you all inside. Now we are all one big family. I will send them back in a couple of days. As you must already know, my dear Ruth, it gives me great pleasure to think about being with you, also.

Lovingly,
Martin

February 16, 1989

Dear friend,

Sometimes when I am very tired and my chest thumps a little, and it feels as though all the wind has been knocked out of me, then I wonder if I will make the long trek back here again. And I know it will be all right. It will not matter if I do not make it back because I will have been here. Then I think about you in prison, and that, too, seems all right. There is a rightness about things as I think about it here, in the quiet middle of the night. What is right is that it doesn't matter what the world does to us. What matters is what we are inside. I see how life gives us tasks and puts us in the best place to grow so that we can eventually be capable of those tasks.

I am thinking of your letters and how they are like a blossom opening. What is in the blossom was once a bud, and before that a seed, and the seed is the condensed person, who has been many times on earth and had many times to experience the things that earth can give us. And all the past is in us still so that we are the things and the places that we have been and seen.

This is a special moment that I am given this night to see just slightly beyond the outer surface—a tiny glimpse of what it might be like to see reality and to know that how it is is all right, to understand a bit that it is all progress—not the moment, fixed, stagnant but everything in movement.

How grateful I am to be able to say such things to you. And I come full circle back to the start of this letter, to think of life and death and how when I die, I will be no farther away than we are now. Perhaps, in a way, even closer. But maybe not, because even now we can be together in sleep, as people are together in death, or when one is dead and the other is alive. What does it matter? When we have learned a new vision, there will be no barrier, and we can be patient until then because love flowing back and forth sustains us.

Right thinking, like appreciating a beautiful sunset, is a contribution to the world. Thoughts and feelings are quite real, and it matters how and what we think and feel even when they are not carried into deeds.

Much love,
Ruth

February 21, 1989

My dearest Ruth,

Today is relatively warm, which is surprising because the last couple of days were extremely cold. During the cold season around here, it gets deathly quiet. I don't know if it's because of the cold weather or what. It may be because the guys are busy trying to keep warm since it has to be raining icicles before the heating system is turned on.

Guess what, the stuffed seal is a beautiful idea. It would give my "room" a touch of character. You wanna know what's even more surprising, I think I could get the guys to go for it! In here, once a person has established himself as being of a certain character, he is usually stuck with it. Of course, the institution doesn't allow such things.

I'm going to let you in on a little secret. When I was about five and six and having no one but sisters to play with, they used to share their baby dolls with me. When I was turning seven, I convinced my parents to let me go and live with my male cousins for the summer. After arriving at my cousins' house, I asked them when we were going to play with the dolls. I'll never forget the looks they gave me. My uncle and aunt had five sons, and we all got along like brothers. I had the best time with them, and when my uncle told me he was going to see if my parents would give their okay to let me stay with them for good, I think I was one of the happiest kids in the world. But when I started thinking of being away from home and my sisters, well, that just didn't sit too well with me and I told my cousins that if my sisters couldn't come and stay also, I didn't want to stay either. Before leaving my cousins' house that summer, they took the liberty of calling me baby doll. Even today my mom tells me, whenever they are asking about me, they still refer to me as baby doll.

Your letter of February 16 is a very beautiful one. It is a good thing that you are helping me with my spiritual education. Otherwise, after reading your letter, I might have thought you to be a little mad, particularly this line: "And I think about you in prison and that, too, seems all right." But, oh how I love you so much for saying that because I know at this moment you are at peace and in tune with all things. These are the moments that I sometimes refer to in my letters as being magical; so you see, my dearest, you're a genie after all!

I think spiritual understanding is so in-depth until it is beyond the norm. This is the exact reason I am beginning to get a lot of strange looks from some of the guys during some of our discussions, because I sometimes say things that only someone like you would be able to understand.

I have been thinking seriously of being a counselor to juvenile delinquents. Since being in prison, I have seen guys come into the system that really didn't need to be here, and after being here a while, they go back into society worse than they were when they came in. With the right kind of counseling, I think a lot of these young guys can be turned in the right direction without the help of prison. Take me, for instance, this is my second time in prison, and up until six and a half months ago—that's when I met you, my love—all I was dwelling on is how to beat the system. Believe me I've had all kinds of counseling, and none of it did any good. Then you came along with your "special something," and I really see the errors of my past ways. You see you really did it with kindness, gentleness, and most of all, with love. How could I resist you? If those three qualities were used in a lot of our counseling methods, I'm sure the number of youths coming into prison would be a lot less.

I send you my blessings with all of my heart. I am beginning to wonder how in the world did I ever make it all this time without you. I am convinced beyond a shadow of a doubt that our meeting was predestined. Isn't that beautiful!!

Love yah always!
Martin

———

February 25, 1989

My dear Martin,

We all need to allow ourselves to cry a little now and then. Your letters make me cry. That you smile to keep from crying made me cry, and also that you take comfort in the thought that as each day passes, it isn't as long as it has been before we meet. This morning I had a special longing to see you, so I kept you in my mind and sent lots of hugs. And I thought how marvelous it is that you are able to change and grow, and what a beautiful soul you are. Whatever is coming forth can only happen because it was already there. It has only been covered up and hidden.

Your doll story reminded me of the time I taught handwork. The children did everything together and in the first grade we taught knitting. One of the boys did exceptionally well. After they got better at it, we knitted dolls and the little boy did a whole family. Then he put a beard on the father and liked it so well that the whole family got beards.

Handwork was an important part of the education program. One thing that results is an appreciation for how things are made and for the fact that so many hands are involved in the things we use daily and take for granted. That is a fine exercise, to think of what is involved in the clothes you wear, the food you eat, the house you live in—the things around you that you use every day. It is good, and important, to have an appreciation for how these things are made, what labor and care goes into them. Then there would be much less stealing and lying. When I had my craft shop, selling to crafts people, I was never given a bad check. If I were dealing with delinquents, I would, more than anything else, give them things to do with their hands.

More love than I know how to express,
Ruth

CHAPTER 4

Old Conditioning Dies Hard

February 26, 1989

My dearest Ruth,

About Mr. Daily's method of directing love and positive thoughts toward those we wish to influence, I don't know why, but it has taken two readings of his book, along with your letters and some remembering of past experiences, to realize that his method works beyond a shadow of a doubt. I remember about two months after my fight with the guards here, I was just sitting in my room wondering what type of person would physically take advantage of a person that's helpless to defend himself. After contemplating along these lines of thought for a while, I tried to put myself in the guards' shoes, and surprisingly, I realized I couldn't do it. After I thought about this for a while, I found out it was because I was harboring too much hate and thoughts of revenge. From my past experiences, hate is a very ugly and evil thing. When a person wastes time hating, he misses out on so many beautiful things! It took me about two weeks to dissolve this hatred and thoughts of revenge long enough to really see things from both sides.

Well, after accomplishing this step, I started concentrating on this one officer in particular, probably because he is more notorious for beating prisoners in handcuffs than the rest of them. After meditating on this officer for a week, I came to the conclusion that he was a sick person. I reasoned that if I were him, I wouldn't want anyone to hate me, but help me instead. When I started seeing this officer as a sick person, I really started feeling sorry for him. Every night I used to send my heart out to him in my prayers, and one night I actually cried for him. I'm so excited telling you about this that my eyes are misty now. Anyway, about two nights later, I was sitting on my bunk daydreaming and I heard someone calling my name. When I looked up at my door, there he was, staring right into my eyes.

Ruth love, if you asked me why, I couldn't tell you, but when I looked up and saw him, I started calling him every profane and cuss word I could think of. You won't believe this, but he really looked hurt and walked away as though he had just lost his best friend. I really felt ashamed of myself after he left. I think he kind of scared me by coming up on me all of a sudden like that. I haven't seen him since, but I'm sure I will sooner or later. I never did connect his coming to my room like that with my meditation, but now, thanks to you, I'm rather sure that's what did it.

I think I might know the Bible just as well as anyone else, which really doesn't help much in the way of spiritual growth. I was living proof before you came into my life. I was practically raised inside of a church, with one of my uncles being the pastor of it. My most vivid memory about the services is wishing all the time that services would get over with so I could get back to shooting marbles.

Love always,
Martin

———————

February 26, 1989

Dear Martin,

I write a letter and marvel at the wonder of being able to put these markings on paper, of it then going into a little mailbox from where it is carried away to find its way to another human being, who can then make out one's thoughts. So many wonders are involved in just this very tiny aspect of modern life, and so many people, more than we can possibly grasp. If we want to stop wars and drugs and poison in agriculture, and all the ways that damage is done to earth and man and life, then one thing can make a great difference and that is to teach every child who enters school about wonder. Wonder, especially in very early childhood, must become the first and highest priority of what we teach. It cannot be done by saying to the child, "Have a sense of wonder," but by teaching in such a way that wonder is part of every aspect of the teaching. It must be taught by teachers who carry such wonder in themselves that it expresses itself in every moment of their lives and therefore in their teaching. They must emanate wonder, and also love—love of earth and of all God's creations. Diane is such a teacher in her kindergarten class, where it should begin, from the very first moment the child's feet carry him/her into a classroom, and blessed are her children for her presence. When they are older, it may be possible to look back and know that at least once during their time in school the classroom was a holy place.

God bless,
Ruth

March 4, 1989

Dear, dear Martin,

Back in Missouri. Now the wait comes again, for the house to sell. But I am patient and accepting of what comes.

Remember how I have been telling you to seem to be your old self around the other inmates, and that you need not tell anyone of your work with love, or your change? Here is a story I have been trying to remember but could not, and it is in an article I came across in a magazine: A cobra goes to a saint and asks for teachings so he can be more spiritual. The saint says, "Well first of all, don't bite people anymore." So the cobra goes back down the mountain, happy that the saint has accepted him as a student, and he sits by the village path all day long, thinking over the saint's advice. After a couple of days, people begin to notice him, and since he's sitting so still and looks so happy, the people get curious. After a few more days, unafraid of the cobra by now, some of the children start poking him with sticks and teasing him, throwing pebbles at him, kicking dirt on his head. And a few cruel adults, too, toss garbage on him and kick him when they walk by. Not long afterward the saint walks by and sees him there all bruised and bloody and full of mud. He says, "My God, what's happened to you?" The cobra replies, "I was just following your instructions, master. I don't bite people anymore." The saint looks down lovingly at the cobra and says, "But I didn't tell you not to hiss!"

And the person writing the article says to a prisoner he's writing this story to, "I know it's tough. I really do. And you don't have to act gentle and wise. Just be yourself—a person who is strong, who ain't gonna take nonsense and is gentle and wise too. But being gentle doesn't mean letting people step all over you. Being wise doesn't mean you always know what to do, or that you never make mistakes."

About your experience with the guard, on which you practiced Mr. Daily's method of directing love, you can see two things—one, that it works, and two, that it is not at all easy to change or even to grasp a new idea. We get stuck in old habits, our old way of thinking and reacting, not really hearing what is said or written. But actually, I am deeply impressed by your understanding, your acceptance of new ideas, your changes, your sensitivity and lovingness.

Thanks, dear Martin, for your fine letters. Thanks for your beautiful poem. Thanks for being you and for writing to me. Thanks for the nice things you say about me. It is important, though, that you know that I am an ordinary lady, who is just as capable as anybody of making mistakes, doing dumb things, saying the wrong thing at the wrong time (a special talent of mine) and of falling "flat on my face" in many ways. But it's OK. I've also learned to accept myself as I am, just as I accept others as they are. I realize I'm a person, too, just as important as any other person and also just as unimportant.

And I love you a whole lot,
Ruth

CHAPTER 5

Prison Violence

March 6, 1989

My dearest Ruth,

I hope my letter finds you in good spirits back in Missouri. I am sitting here trying to figure out how to begin telling you about this past, tragic week. I suppose I'd better start from the beginning. You know, sometimes when things really bad are going to happen to me, I always get this feeling inside of me— it's like a warning of doom or something that always comes over me about two or three days before it happens, and I find it very unfortunate that I haven't paid it any attention until now.

Remember the guard that I mentioned in my last letter—the notorious prisoner beater? As fate would have it, I had another meeting with him on March 1. It began and ended like this: Every week, if the weather permits, the guys in confinement are taken outside for two hours of fresh air by the guards that work this building. Well, for some mysterious reason this officer happened to be one of the guards taking us outside that afternoon.

Before each inmate is let out of his cell, he is handcuffed behind his back. When all of the inmates were out of their cells and standing in the hallway, an inmate started complaining to the guards that his handcuffs were too tight and one of the guards told him to shut up before he locks him back in his cell. Me and about five other inmates spoke up on the inmate's behalf. Suddenly everybody's attention was directed at the notorious officer, and he was looking directly at me, screaming shut up. Something inside of me was yelling, "Go back to your cell, go back to your cell," because after looking in his eyes I knew I had fallen into a trap. But to beg them to put me back in my cell would have been a cowardly thing to do in the eyes of the inmates and guards alike, so I just shut my mouth and started praying that my premonition was wrong.

As we were being escorted down the hallway and downstairs to the recreational yard the officer grabbed the back of my handcuffs and brutally snatched me to him. I suppressed my anger and asked him what was wrong. He told me he was personally going to take my handcuffs off. After all the other handcuffs were off and the prisoners were let through the gate into the yard, they just stood at the gate watching to see what would happen. The officer proceeded to take my cuffs off and after they were off I politely thanked him, grateful that the situation wasn't going any further than it already had. I took about six steps toward the gate and I heard him say in a guttural tone, "Come back here Forrest!" I knew then that my earlier premonition was right. With all of my heart I wanted to pretend I didn't hear this guy, but to ignore him would be considered an act of open rebellion, which would give them the right to use whatever force they wished to restrain a rebellious prisoner.

When I turned around and started walking toward him, I was desperately trying to look as humble as a lamb, hoping this would let him know that I didn't want to fight him or anybody else. I asked him as humbly as I could what was wrong, and he looked at me with an intimidating look and said, "I'm taking your recreation period for verbally disrespecting an officer, and I'm giving you a verbal order to put your hands behind your back to be handcuffed." The other inmates started protesting because they had also read the set-up. It's a common practice for the guards here to accuse you of something, handcuff you, and beat you into a coma.

If it had been any other guard besides this one that gave the order, I might have considered it, but not for this guy because he was looking too evil. It was the same look he had on his face the last time he gave me this order and I foolishly obeyed and ended up in the hospital having an operation. I made up my mind then, if I was going to be brutally beaten again, it sure wasn't going to happen with my hands behind my back. He looked at me as though I had just openly defied God, and he drew back his hand and slapped me. It's times like these that I fear the most, because I get so mad that I can only see blackness. By the time he drew back to slap me again, the other guards started running toward us and the prisoners started scaling the fence to help me. When the other guards saw the prisoners coming over the fence like demons, they backed off. When the smoke cleared, the officer was lying on the concrete in a puddle of blood and I wasn't bleeding anywhere.

Ruth, I can't say anything in this letter for fear of incriminating myself because I am being charged with battery on a correctional officer, so I will have to fill you in on the details of that particular incident after my trial. After we were taken back to our cells, the guards came to my cell and whipped me unconscious and for a minute there I thought I was dead. When I realized I wasn't, I had to pretend I was to stop the beating. When the guards realized I'd stopped moving, I think it kind of frightened them a little, so they rushed me to the hospital.

After the doctor got through sewing up my face and head injuries, I was placed in one of the hospital rooms for twenty-four hours observation until I could be transferred to a medical facility to take x-rays and a cat scan to make sure I didn't have any internal injuries. After the x-rays and cat scan, I was transferred to the highest maximum security prison in the state.

You wanna hear something funny?! When the prisoners started scaling the fence, the guards started yelling "Freeze! Freeze!" When the prisoners kept coming, the guards started looking around for a place to run, but there was no place to run to. I saw the same blood lust in the inmates' eyes that I had seen in the guards' eyes and the guards were outnumbered five to one with the inmates advancing. I remembered that the prisoners had come over the fence to help me and I realized that if somebody didn't do something fast, these five guards were going to get killed. Suddenly I started yelling for everybody to be cool; there was no sense in things going any farther than they already had, because if it did, a lot of us were going to end up on death row. Things got deathly quiet. Then I told the guards that if they would kindly open the door, we would all go back to our cells voluntarily. The funny part is, instead of the guards thanking me, they were acting as though they wanted to kill me!

You see, Ruth, in an explosive situation like the one I just described, when inmates will listen to another inmate instead of the guards, then that inmate is considered dangerous in the eyes of the guards, because they know that if it hadn't been for me, all of them would probably be dead. By the same token, I could have said "Let's kill them," and they would be dead. Fortunately for me and the guards, I don't harbor that kind of hatred for them or anyone else. More than anyone else, the guards and I should be thanking you, my dear Ruth, because I realize and understand so clearly that if I hadn't met you and regenerated myself, I know in my heart that I gladly would have led the slaughter on those five guards. Now, more than ever, I am forever grateful to you! Isn't it strange, when we start to think we have everything in order as far as life goes, life turns around and plays a cruel trick on us in the form of tragedy!

I'm wondering what it all means, where is all of this leading to? Ahh, but thanks to you, something tells me I already have the answer. When I try to see it with the naked eye, I am blind, and when I try to hear it with the human ear, I am deaf. I will now look in a place where few of us would ever think to look, within my soul.

I want you to know that I am not sitting here pining away, nor do I look upon my yesterdays with regret, but rather as valuable lessons for all of my tomorrows!

I send you endless love,
Martin

P.S. All of my stamps and other important papers got soaked in blood, and this is one of the reasons it's taken me so long to write to you. The other reason is I had to wait until my eyes opened back up because they were swollen shut. And tonight is free letter night. If I seem to be repeating myself, or not making a lot of sense, please bear with me because my eyes are still slightly shut and feel like they are on fire. I can never thank you enough for being my friend. Thank you! Love!

March 7, 1989

My dearest Ruth,

This letter is more or less the second part of the other one. I think I am writing a little better today because I'm not as shaky as I was yesterday. One of the guards was trying to break my arms by bending them behind my head, but all he succeeded in doing was unbalancing my equilibrium and causing a lot of soreness. Right now they have me so far back in one of these confinement cells that I can't tell night from day. Not that I am complaining, mind you, because that's just a waste of energy.

The investigating lieutenant at this institution wanted to know what I promised the prisoners to make them obey me like that rather than the officers. The question caught me completely by surprise and I could only look at him stupidly. It might interest you to know that I haven't answered the question yet. I think I might know the answer, but I'm not yet able to put it into words. Maybe you can help me?

I am suddenly reminded of one of your poems: the part about life cares not whether we say no to its lessons, they just keep coming back until we learn from them. Well, I was just laughingly thinking I had better learn from this one because I don't think I can stand another like this too soon. You know, once a mind understands the destructive forces of hate, the useless, time-consuming energy wasted on trying to intensify this passion when we could be building a more constructive world, then it becomes almost impossible to hate someone no matter what they may do to you. And I am speaking from experience, dear lady. Thank you! "I have learned silence from the talkative, tolerance from the intolerant and kindness from the unkind. I should not be ungrateful to those teachers."—Kahlil Gibran. I cannot thank Mr. Gibran enough for this beautiful enlightenment. You see, Ruth love, unknowingly the guards taught me a valuable lesson concerning brutality.

There is a wild conversation going on right now about the incident that happened last week between me and the guards. The prisoners here are trying to champion me as a hero. But don't worry, I wouldn't dare let their praise inflate my ego because I have perceived this to be vanity. I am more convinced now than ever how effective our thoughts are concerning our everyday lives and the people around us. I shall start using my thoughts in a more constructive manner from this point on. I think I'd better close my letter for now because my eyes are beginning to burn again. Perhaps they'll get better when the swelling goes down.

Take care and remember I love you always!
Martin

———————————

March 10, 1989

My very dear Martin,

First of all I want to tell you how very grateful I am that you could speak to me so frankly in the two letters I just received. It is important for you to be able to write it and for me to hear it. It is one thing to know that it goes on in the world and quite another to discover that it is happening to someone you love. I cannot stop crying, not only for you, but for the world in general. But I will have to stop for a little while because I want to send this letter today, and for that I have to go to the post office as today's mail has already been picked up. In fact, it was the delivery that brought your letters. And I'll also send a money order in case you have need of it. I don't know how much, so I'll send the usual ten. Let me know if you need more. Call me if you need it soon, or if ever you need to call, I know it will have to be collect.

What can I say except I admire and love you very much. A person would have to be clairvoyant to understand the meaning of it, and I am not. Nothing comes to me except pain and numbness. How typical of certain people to react as the guards did to your saving their lives. It is so hard to realize that people do not really think or that their reaction to things is so twisted. I have had similar experiences, in a much milder way, when people I helped turned on me because their low, low egos were hurt.

I can't think of anything to say except to pray for guidance. You can be sure you will be in my prayers constantly. Something that you can sense before it happens, if it is pre-ordained, has got to have a special meaning and/or purpose. I wish so much to be able to see you. We shall have to do it in sleep.

I shall stop now and go out while the sun is still up. I think I can stop crying until I get back. We funny people!

So much love, my darling,
Ruth

———————

March 10, 1989

Dearest,

It is later. The earlier letter has been mailed, and I did some shopping while I was out. I've been having pain in one hip. It started in California and has gotten worse. It's bad now, along with a good deal of general achiness, so I got enough food for a longish stretch in case it takes a while to clear up. I shall postpone a trip to friends in Memphis, Tennessee. I had something like it a while ago, on the other side, and found no help, so I shall patiently wait it out. I'm allergic to drugs of any kind, and when I went to a doctor last time, the treatment only increased the pain. So I'll have a quiet, restful time, which is what helps, and in my own way, unintentionally, I shall be sharing a little of your pain though I know yours is far worse.

The crying seems to be over, not the soul pain, and maybe still a tear now and then, as I think of you. I'm thinking of how you were able to restrain the prisoners and what I say can only be in the form of questions. Perhaps it made a difference that you know how prisoners think and react? Maybe it is because they know you care about them? Maybe they respect you?

I am remembering how you recently spoke of ignorance. That certainly plays a big role. I had the idea that guards should be taught how to be guards, and the next thought was, who shall teach them? I have to say again what I have said before. These are not enlightened times; they are the darkest of times. The best thing a person can do is become enlightened. One at a time, it will eventually build up and have an effect.

I have been trying to send love to everyone involved in this insanity, and how difficult it is! Each time I am overwhelmed with sadness. I keep seeing in my mind the prisoners approaching the guards. It is like a war about to happen. In an actual war, they might be looked upon as heros, but anything that is out of control, where intelligence is no longer operative, is scary.

I told you in an earlier letter that I would try to describe what works, along with love, and I don't think it is anything one can put on and wear like a garment. It is what one becomes. It is being sure of what is good and right. It is wanting to be truly helpful. It is caring for all who are involved. It is practicing Christianity, which did not prevent Christ from being crucified. It is understanding what Gandhi understood, even if you might make different decisions. It is a kind of inner confidence. It is standing upright and sure in your own soul. It is being kind and trying to live all this with love.

Again, I send you much love,
Ruth

———

March 11, 1989

Beloved friend,

I still wonder how much was destined, how much could have been avoided? It is the way of present day thinking to imagine you must have offered the prisoners something to stop them. Well, perhaps in a subtle way you did. Maybe it is in being in sympathy with them and in caring.

I have had to deal with negative things with a good many people in my lifetime—with selfishness, thoughtlessness, ignorance, anger, various emotions—but cruelty and brutality for its own sake are not among them. I am finding it especially difficult to send love in this case but am working at it. You, I surround with protective and healing light.

Much love,
Ruth

March 15, 1989

My very dearest Ruth,

It was my intention to ask you please don't cry. But I will ask
you instead that if you must cry for me, let your cry be of joy.
Rejoice in the knowledge that a soul like me was lost, but now
I am found. I was blind, but now I see. We will both cry for
the souls who are lost and will not see, because as they are
now, the world is set on a course where we can do nothing
but go backward instead of forward. It is just as a great man
once said, "We must all come together as one or perish."

I thank you very much for sending your phone number in
my time of crisis, but part of my punishment is that I'm not
allowed any phone calls. You need not worry because I know
that you are forever with me. It is times like these that I am
most comforted with the thought that the Lord will never give
us more than we can bear. The worst thing that could happen
to me is for me to allow myself to be reduced to a vengeful
and hateful state like I did the first time this happened.

I told you about the time I was beaten, and how I spent two
months after that plotting vengeance. For a long time after the
first incident, all I could think of was revenge, all I could
breathe and talk about was revenge. Surely if Christ was able
to forgive his persecutors, I can easily forgive my ignorant
brothers or not be ungrateful to my brutal teachers. To whom
much is given much is required. By the magical wonderments
of the angels and the graces of your charitable heart, I have
been given much understanding and love. Now it is required
of me to give to those who are without and I shall start with
my brutal teachers. It has come to me that love, wisdom, and
understanding should not only be assimilated with the intellect
but with the soul as well. When these three qualities of truth
are not merely in my brain, but are assimilated in my being as
well, only then will I be able to vouch for their meaning with
people like my brutal teachers, and this is what I am meditating
on daily.

It seems that no matter how hard we strive in earnestness
to become more than what we are, there always will be visible
and invisible forces of hindrance. Do you reckon this could be
to make our convictions stronger? You don't need to answer
that because I'm only wondering out loud. You know some-

thing, you're great, and I love you very much! Please give the family my love and hello's.

Love yah!
Martin

CHAPTER 6

First Memory

March 16, 1989

My very dear Martin,

I know that worry is not helpful—in fact, that it can make things more difficult, yet I now know that I have been your mother (and mothers worry). It was through experiencing your recent difficulty as a mother would experience it, that the memory was awakened. It explains so much that I carried in my feelings for you. For instance, in the beginning, I could only see you as a child of about ten, not black, not that it matters as you well know, but it was the only vision I could conjure up of you. And now I know that to be very real. It is so very important to "put you in God's hands" and to have faith and trust in what is given to us. I have felt, since we started writing, that you are in training for a future task. I saw you only as the very beautiful, gentle, loving soul who was my son so very long ago. Now, suddenly, it is even more difficult to see you with objectivity. Being a mother is quite different from a friend. Everything is felt so much more deeply. One can feel the mother/child connection in a real way even when it is a relationship from the past. And ours was so very special.

I worry—even knowing that I must not—about not hearing from you since the two letters over a week ago, telling me of the incident. Hopefully there will be a letter in the next mail. Yes, we must meet and talk one day. I cannot imagine it otherwise. I think how amazing it is that the authorities there look upon you as violent and dangerous, yet you are one of the gentlest of souls. You have my love and caring and blessing. What sets you apart is your work on yourself. Continuing that, humbly, is the best that we can do. And now this is the best that I can do.

With so very much love,
Ruth

———————

March 18, 1989

Dear, dear Martin,

Your letter of March 15 just came, and it has put me at ease about you. Thank you so much. Now you are my teacher. I'm afraid I reacted like a mother (and a Jewish mother, at that) and forgot all the things I had been telling you. I can see now how I have been seeing you from that unconscious memory of the past, and for the first time, I am able to look at the present and finally see you as "of a dark complexion," as you said. I can sort of put the past back in the past and make a new connection with you as you are now.

I am so pleased about our past connection. It was very beautiful, full of love and goodness and an appreciation of nature—what we still have. We were very much in tune and needed no words to communicate. It doesn't seem surprising that we are so in tune now. How very special you are, and how special to me!

I love you so very much,
Ruth

———————

March 19, 1989

My dearest Ruth,

I hope you aren't experiencing unbearable pain in your hip. As for me, the only problem I'm having is with my left arm. I'm sure it's not broken, but whenever I try to stretch it all the way out, I experience pain. I think the joints are out of place. Given a little time and patient exercising it will probably be back to normal. My eyes are doing very well, and I had the stitches taken out of my head a couple of days ago. So you see, I'm really recovering quite well and am sending get well thoughts your way.

History has demonstrated that to free a man it is not enough to strike the shackles from his limbs, his mind must be liberated from bondage to his own ignorance. You have stated it eloquently when you say that a person needs to become enlightened. Without that I would be facing more serious charges than I am facing now, and I have you to thank for that.

I am going to attempt to answer your question as humbly and honestly as I can: How much was destined, how much could have been avoided? Three or four days before the incident took place, I had this feeling of dread come over me that something bad was going to happen. After thinking on it for a while, I dismissed the whole idea as nothing. Three days later that officer showed up. It had occurred to me to refuse to go to recreation, but I like to face a problem head on and not duck it. Once in the hallway I could have asked to be allowed to go back to my cell, but then I would have been looked upon as a coward, not only by the prisoners and the guards, but by myself as well. To sum it all up, it was like choosing to live a life of cowardly shame or dying a heroic death. I chose death.

Lovingly,
Martin

———

March 20, 1989

My very dear Martin,

The enclosed letter arrived today. Because of the inefficiency of the post office, it was delayed, and this time I'm grateful. If it had come before your letters, I really would have been in a panic. He did the right thing, of course. His letter shows real concern and a desperate plea to get help for you. The letter was addressed to Carmel, and they messed up on forwarding it although I had left the proper cards. Thank God!

Please let me know what could be done or who I might get information from in the future, even though I certainly hope there is never another incident. What about court proceedings? What do you do about a lawyer? I haven't asked before because

I feel like a helpless bystander. I've only prayed a lot. And I have to say this is the most difficult experience of trying to love the unlovable that I have ever had. I admire the way you are dealing with it. You say all the right things in your letter to help me, too.

March 21—I spoke about how, when we ask earnest questions, we get answers. I awoke in the middle of the night thinking about you, and I pictured myself going into your cell and sitting with you in meditation. I actually could go beyond the barriers that had kept me from loving your attackers. I could feel love for them. And then I realized that Christ sat with us and that, through His being, that kind of love became possible. Each of us alone may find it difficult or impossible, but together, two or more in His name, it is much more possible. But you had already done it, and then I could join you. And when I want to experience it again, I go back and join you in your cell, which is, at the moment, a spiritual place.

It is good to see the list of those who care and are ready to support you. I am writing to the man who wrote to me to thank him very much.

Bless you, dear friend, you are much loved,
Ruth

March 2, 1989 (received March 20)
Ms Ruth:

I am a direct associate of Forrest, and I am writing to let you know he was, along with several other inmates including myself, in the process of attending the recreation yard at which time this same particular officer that had previously assaulted him perpetrated another attack for apparently no reason.

He is in the hospital under observation where his privilege of communicating with outside support could possibly be restricted because of external or internal injuries he's suffering from due to the assault.

I am pretty sure he would sincerely appreciate your concerned interest to contact his relatives, if known, as well as this institution in an effort to obtain a reading, I mean a thorough reading of his physical condition.

From my position, I cannot provide you with a personal accounting of his condition, but according to an officer's account, he is in pretty bad shape. So, my advice would be to contact this institution or the Secretary, Office of the Department of Corrections, immediately.

Ms. Ruth I am going to include a list of names of the inmates that can be very helpful to him; they witnessed the entire incident that brought about the assault, so be sure to forward the names and their numbers to him because he will be needing them since the institution may have charged him to cover their own dirty tracks. Be sure he gets these names, OK?

May God bless and keep you within his everlasting guidance. Amity.

March 21, 1989

My beloved friend,

Today I was brought out of the dark cell and placed in a regular one, and I am not sure which one I like the best. I find it amazing and wonderfully magical how we as humans are gifted with the ability to take punishment and turn it into a blessing. I have heard it said that for those who have the eyes to see, nothing is concealed, for those who have the right to know, all things are open books. I am prepared to say, at this very moment, that all things are blessing if we are receptive to them.

It is Tuesday and evening is near, darkness is descending upon the earth, and everything seems to have taken on a more tranquil form. As I look out of my window, I am thinking of you. I am wondering who is this woman who has the magical powers to raise a soul like me from the depths of hell to the heights of eternal bliss and enlightenment? Who is this woman who inspires in me the quality to want to reach out to the world and say, "I love you," to reach out to my enemies with understanding and say, "I love you and forgive you, and if you will only open your eyes, you will see that we are one." The woman who I speak of—her name is Ruth. Her language is universal and is understood only by those who have allowed themselves to hear. Perhaps, one day in the not too distant future, we will all speak her language, which will make for a better world.

I am now in a confinement cell block area with several other guys in single cells. The guy next door to me sings at the top of his voice, and what a terrible voice he has!

I also find it difficult to try to send love to my brutal teachers.

Whenever I relive the scene over in my mind, I tend to get angry, but then I follow Rudolf Steiner's suggestion in *Knowledge of the Higher Worlds* about going to the mountaintop and looking down from a distance, objectively, and the problem is made less difficult. Why anybody would want to inflict pain and brutality on others is beyond the both of us, but I am sure you would agree that these are the ones who need the most help.

Have a happy Easter!

I love you dearly,
Martin

March 22, 1989

My beloved Ruth,

There isn't any more bad news. The absence of mail from me was due to the extensive legal research I was doing last week. I am trying to prepare a legal defense for any assault charges since the day of the incident and that's the day they read me my rights. I could have sued them and won convincingly after the last incident, but I didn't because of my new way of being and that is practicing love and forgiveness. They obviously didn't know my reason for not suing, but I am sure they are aware that it is still not too late. Perhaps they fear I will use this suit as a leverage against them and that is why they are taking so long deciding what to do. I have faith that things will end well for all parties concerned. It is training for all it's worth.

The weather is fine, not too hot or too cold. The window is too far from my cell for me to get a clear view of the outside, but I can see cars in the far distance as they pass by.

Lovingly,
Martin

March 23, 1989

My dearly beloved,

I hope you can imagine the joy, happiness, and enthusiasm you have given me at your newfound discovery—a mother's worry. I have always felt, from the beginning of our letters, that there was a special bond between us. You see, all of my life the words, "I love you," have been a hard thing for me to say to anyone, including my immediate family. It felt like I would be taking a chance with the most vulnerable part of my being, and it always seemed to get stuck in my throat. And then came your first letter. It felt so wonderful, so light. It was magic. After reading your letter, I could feel a special aura emanating from it, and I smiled a deep smile from within, because, for reasons I cannot explain, I knew within my soul that I could trust you enough to say I love you without it being a gamble. And it has been this way for me ever since that first letter.

I shall always keep you informed, my love, so you need not worry yourself. I love you very much! I am feeling kind of poetic tonight and your letter is responsible, so here it is. You make me very happy. I have been sitting here in a daze of joy and happiness, smiling at the walls. I want to say something to you with words that words cannot express. I guess I'll have to settle for "I love you" and send you my heart.

Poem

For the grace of your love have I been made whole;
For the grace of your tenderness my love is no longer cold.
Feeling and understanding has allowed me to shed tears;
There are still times I am afraid to cry, but thinking of you conquers
    these fears.
I am scorned by the weak and laughed at by fools,
When it is only for them that I shed these tears.
By their scorn and laughter am I strengthened
Because their understanding is nil;
It is only by their vices am I shown the Father's will.

To Ruth with love,
Martin

March 24, 1989

Dear, dear Martin,

I smile at your letter, which says such nice things about a quite ordinary lady, and I send you a big hug. My health is truly better. I am my old hobbling self, able to use my legs a bit with the help of the cane.

I'm glad you are out of the dark cell and hope the guy with the terrible voice doesn't sing a lot or that you can maybe stuff cotton in your ears.

I love to recall the old memory of our past connection. It is so clear. I see you as a young boy, about ten, gentle, helpful, amazingly understanding, wise, loving. Between us there was something especially deep and beautiful. Some catastrophe, which I can't see, shortened all our lives, your sister and father, also. I have always, since we started writing, had a hard time seeing you as in your late twenties and black. It is a bit easier now to separate the past from the present, but still the old memory is very strong. I, too, feel with you your description of sitting in a daze of joy, smiling at the walls. Your letters still make me cry because they are so special, and also, I suppose, because something from the past still lives within me.

Love always,
Ruth

April 5, 1989

Dearest love,

I was surprised by the many names on the letter you received from my friend because most guys usually don't like to get involved in matters such as this for fear of repercussions from the institution. It is also against institutional policies for inmates to write to each other from one institution to the other. Considering how prisoners usually shy away from situations like this, I owe all of these guys the highest honor and my deepest thanks.

The four books you sent with my package permit arrived. I like them all. Do you think it strange for someone to be in a cell twenty-four hours around the clock and sometimes still not have enough time to do all the things he wants to do in one day? That's me. I told a guy that last week and he replied, "Man, are you crazy."

The value that I place on these books, and all the other writings you send me, is beyond measure and I am forever grateful. Thank you! You are truly a mother, and my heart is overwhelmed with love for you, always.

A guy and I were discussing freedom late last night, and he gave me the impression that he thought freedom is total irresponsibility. I immediately reverted to some of the questions you posed to me and suddenly it became much clearer what you were saying, and oh, how right you are! Freedom must make sense. All things must be governed by laws or else they will exist in a perpetual state of nonsense, chaos, and destruction, and I cannot imagine that as freedom.

I am enclosing my parents' address and phone number. From this point on, I shall start filling you in on me and my family's relationship. The love is naturally there on both sides, but I don't think we know each other very well. I am doing my best to try to correct that. I wouldn't dare expose some of my feelings to them as I do to you because they wouldn't understand. The beautiful thing is that our relationship has improved drastically since I met you and that is another reason why you are so very special to me.

Lovingly,
Martin

April 7, 1989

My very dear Martin,

To say "I give you my heart" is certainly to love without fear. And that is very beautiful! Sometimes someone will do that to someone who later betrays that love and trust, or seems to, and then it is important to know that the love has been great, no matter what. Do not be sorry to have so loved. I say that because one must not be fearful about loving. Christ has done it, and Gandhi, and Schweitzer, and so many, many others. You will be in good company. I suppose everyone has had some sort of painful experience with love. Love is the greatest lesson on earth. When a lot more people learn it, the earth will be a better place. One of the sayings attributed to Gandhi is that "one person who truly loves can undo the hate of many."

Since so few books are allowed, I will try to send you reading materials in other ways, along with my letters. Some will be parts of books, copied on my copier. In some instances, you may eventually get all the parts. They do not permit magazines, either. One was returned to me. I am sending a copied article, hoping that might be acceptable.

Know that my thoughts and prayers and love are ever with you,
Ruth

———

April 26, 1989

My beloved Ruth,

Like the cool winds and rains give soothing comfort to the parched earth, so are you a comfort to me. You have given me magical wonderments. Once I only had the urge to understand the relative, but now I crave the absolute. Surely you have looked into my soul and have seen the hunger of one who has only lived in the shadows of proper nourishment. You have given your ears to the cries of the child who moans from within for fear of being laughed at by those who would even make fun of their God, whom they have not known. With arms of compassion, you have embraced the profane, who in return now wishes to be reunited with the eternal who dwells in the heights of love, wisdom, and understanding. I am that I am! My shame and nakedness have you cloaked with the garments of truth and behind the walls of imprisonment your wisdom has made me free. The tongue that would stutter have you made a speaker in the universal language that all can understand but might not speak. To the eyes have you given the vision to look beyond the density of the physical body and absorb the universal being. My hell have you taken away by removing the veil of ignorance and death. Only now can it truly be said that I have been given a choice. I thank you so very much, my beautiful Ruth, for giving me a choice.

As I was lying down last night, I began reading *The Prophet* by Kahlil Gibran. A feeling so beautiful came upon me that I could barely contain it. In my excitement, I could not continue to lie down. My whole being was screaming—wow! What a book! I am still chuckling at my silliness. Only you can do this to me. Anyway the book is so inspiring that I am sending you another poem. It is my way of saying thank you with all my heart for giving me life.

Much love,
Martin

———

April 30, 1989

My beloved Ruth,

I am thinking of my family and how at one time I stopped writing to them because they hardly ever write back, and to prove to myself that I really didn't need anyone, I quit writing altogether even though I know they cannot read or write very well. Me and my parents were never really close anyway, so not hearing from them didn't really bother me like it should have.

When I was growing up, I almost ended up hating them forever in my ignorance. I think they made surviving harder than it really was. Even when I was a toddler I remember picking apples, oranges, and working in different types of vegetable fields as a way of survival. I didn't mind the work at all, and I used to hear my parents brag about how much money we were always making for the week and then my father would end up losing it all at a card table. The household bills were never paid and sometimes the electric company would come and turn the lights out. Me and my sisters went hungry a lot of nights because of my father's gambling habits. My mother, in her frustration, would give me some of the fiercest beatings for the least thing, so I grew up being afraid of her. When one lives in a constant state of fear, they hardly have room to love anyone. My mother always used to tell us how much she loved us, and I remember thinking, when she would say this, "What would it be like if she ever starts to hating?" Even though I was kind of afraid of her, her saying she loved us very much made my heart warm with love for her in return and then at my next beating, I'd end up hating myself for loving her. Who knows, maybe I deserved a lot of the beatings because it got to the point where I would go out of my way to do things to make her mad at me so I could show her that her beatings really didn't bother that much. But Lord knows, that wasn't true because I started running away from home at the age of eleven just to avoid her. I never ran very far because I didn't have any place to run to, and when I started thinking of my sisters and how dark it was outside, along with my hunger pains, home sounded like the best place to be.

I could never really stay angry with my parents very long because somehow I always knew that in so many ways they were only kids themselves, who were suddenly saddled with a big parental responsibility which they were not psychologically or emotionally equipped to handle. Considering the average poverty-stricken families during that time, I think we made out quite well because a lot of the kids I grew up with are either dead or strung out on drugs.

You know something, it wasn't until I met you that I really started trying to understand my childhood, my parents, other people and their problems, and life in general. You gave me back more than that which had been taken away from me a long time ago. As I think of you, my heart and soul swells with a love so great that it's almost unbearable. In spite of it all, life for me has always been beautiful because I have learned something from life. I have been a liar, bully, and thief, among other things. As you once asked, "Which of us is really innocent?" You and I are among the most richly blessed, "For I tell you that many prophets and kings have desired to see those things which we see, and have not seen them, and hear the things which we hear and have not heard them." —St. Luke 10:24.

I want to thank you for the enlightening literature that you send me. It teaches me more and affects me more in spiritual ways than the Bible and other teachings ever could. In a short time you have brought me peace that even I have denied myself. You have carried me over mountains that I thought were too high to climb and you've walked with me the desolate roads that I feared to walk alone.

When I think of some of the close brushes I've had with death, I still shudder because by all rights I should have been dead.

You can probably tell by my last couple of letters that I have received your beautiful and much welcomed instructions on how to improve the grammatical structure of my letters. Thank you very much.

Lovingly,
Martin

———————

May 8, 1989

My dearest Ruth,

I think spring is here in full bloom because the weather is mild and cool. It was so hot a couple of weeks ago that I spent most of the day wishing I was in Iceland.

I went to outside court last week to be arraigned for assault and battery charges on a correctional officer. I don't know why, but every time I walk into a courtroom, I get so nervous that I have to psych myself out to remain calm. It seems that I should have outgrown this stage by now since I practically grew up inside of courthouses.

A courtroom has a way of making me feel like a sacrificial lamb. I always get the feeling that the outcome has already been decided and we are only going through the motions of a trial as a symbol of justice for all. No matter how pious the judge, jury and my lawyer, or public defender, seem to be I always end up feeling like I've just been conned. When I stood before the judge and he asked me how do I plead, I refused to say anything because for me to plead guilty would be like putting my head in the lion's mouth and hoping for mercy. The judge tried to get me to speak up, but I maintained my silence, so he entered a not guilty plea for me, pending trial.

Upon entering my cell, an aura of calmness came upon me. Something seemed to be telling me that if I would continue to follow the path that has been set before me, then I can continue to dwell in the kingdom of peace and calmness. Even though

I get a little weak and weary sometimes, I still know that when God is with us the whole world together can't do us any harm. Thanks to you, this fact has been embedded in my heart and soul.

The letter you sent to the warden of this prison obviously has the power to move mountains, because I'm suddenly allowed to receive prison library books, and also ones on loan from an interlibrary loan system.

Sometimes I get the idea that you can read my mind. For instance, sometimes I can be puzzling over a certain matter and you'll suddenly send me some literature or give me the answer in a letter. And sometimes when something is bothering me deeply, I think of you and am bothered no more.

Sometimes thinking of you brings me so much joy that I could just cry.

I love you so very, very much and more,
Martin

Note: My letter to the warden about books was passed on to a superintendent, with whom I carried on a short exchange. He was not cooperative, and, therefore, I was surprised to learn that Martin had been given access to the library. I did not ask for special privileges for him but was concerned at the general policy of not allowing prisoners to better themselves through books and education.

The gesture of allowing him to have books was soon sabotaged by the various library personnel and I could only come to the conclusion that they had played this game in order to put me off. Their method was to claim that he had lost the first two books he'd asked for. One did not even get to him—only the information that he had not returned it and, therefore, had lost his library privileges. At my suggestion (and I sent him the money for this), he offered to pay for them. Their answers were either in the form of gibberish, having nothing to do with the situation at all, or there was simply no answer. We gave up trying to fight this closed system that obviously was going to have it their way. We did not know at that time, and could not even conceive of such a possibility, that in their minds education, or even having books, constituted a threat to their system—their absolute power and their unquestionable authority.—R.S.

May 11, 1989

Dearest Martin,

Sometimes I feel a bit odd when I call you son because you have a mother, and she is your mother of this life. I would never want to take her place. So, perhaps, I can have second place next to her because I was once, also, your mother. And even though we cannot speak to her of such things, maybe she would not mind.

I am thinking of the court proceedings you have to go through, and what you are doing seems to me to be wise. Now I'm going to act like a mother and give you some advice that you probably won't need. Prayer is most important, as you know, always with the idea of "Thy Will Be Done!" If one can manage to be peaceful and have faith and trust, then one can be inspired by the good beings to say the right things. I see them taking you in irons and it used to make me cry, but suddenly it seems crazy and I laugh. It is so ridiculous.

There are so few errors in your letter, I'm very impressed. And you write so well. I see improvement all the time, in every way.

I have been thinking about some of my remarks to you—for instance, about your having to be in shackles when taken out of your room. I can understand why they feel they must do it. From their point of view, they have reason to fear you or your anger. The point, from my point of view, is how little we know of one another. I see your gentle, loving side, they see violence. I see something behind the violence (provocation) that when it is not there, there is no violence. But there is in it an important lesson, and it is to learn not to be violent no matter what anyone (and the world) does to you. I think that is what the spirit world, what Christ, wants us to learn and to become. Then the outer restraints will not be necessary because we will have our own inner restraints. When that time comes, it will be impossible for people to harm each other. For now, the difference must be in whether the anger blindly controls us, or in whether it becomes a tool that we can use when it is needed. And how difficult it is to know the difference!

So I close for now. When I think of being locked up as you are all the time, then I try to keep you supplied with whatever comes to hand to amuse, to stimulate, or to activate your thinking. One must take from one's circumstances whatever good can be extracted, like this time you have to be alone (in a way).

I send you love, lots of love,
Ruth

––––––––––––

May 11, 1989

My dearest Ruth,

I have just finished reading your book again, and I no longer wonder why I love you so very much. I shudder when I think how very sick and lost I was in my thinking and ways of doing things without knowing the degree, nature, or cause of the sickness.

There are some former friends of mine who I vowed to kill, if I ever got out of prison, because they lied against me in the courts to keep themselves out of trouble for crimes they committed. These were the same guys who had taken the loot from some of my robbery ventures to pay their light bills, rent, and to buy food for their kids. It was not because they couldn't find work but wouldn't, and now that I think of them, they were cowards as well as thieves. Yet, if it weren't for these same fellows, I would be dead by now. Can you imagine the conflicting thoughts and changes one goes through when beginning the task of consciously liberating oneself from the bondages of ignorance and death? Of course you can!

Well, one of the hardest fights I've had so far in my personal redemption process is accepting the idea that I should be thankful to these same guys rather than ungrateful. I think it is only right that I tell you that it was only by your love and guidance that I came to face and accept the truth of the matter with a gladness that almost seems insane. It was my acceptance of the absolute truth that made me so very happy that night because a great burden had been lifted. It felt as though I was set free from a task that I did not want to do, but felt compelled to do because of commitment through ignorance.

The happiness and great love I felt that night was the inspiration to the words in the poem "For the Grace of Your Love." It was on that night that I felt a real sense of forgiveness, and the naked realization that, unless we can truly learn to forgive others, it is impossible to forgive ourselves and experience the eternal forgiveness of the holy of all holies.

Lovingly,
Martin

_____

May 21, 1989

My dearest Ruth,

Once again you have astonished me with your ability to know when I am trying to overcome certain obstacles such as anger. There are five other guys in this confinement section besides myself. We are supposedly the elite of the meanest and hardest core prisoners in the state. We are allowed out of our cells one at a time on Mondays, Wednesdays, and Fridays to take a five-minute shower. The security measures they take in bringing us out of our cells would make you swear we are all highly trained assassins. I grant you this—when considered objectively—it is very funny but not in every case.

When you wrote your letter, there were two guys I was having a hectic time with, trying to control my anger. I get along with both of them beautifully, but they hate each other's guts. One is Oriental, the other black. They each try to sway me toward his dislike for the other. It gets so ridiculous sometimes that when I am talking with one, the other will start screaming at the top of his voice to drown him out. Every day seems to be a repeat, and I am beginning to wonder if I was purposely put in the midst of them so they could drive me crazy. (Smile)

Every day I try to apply some of the exercises and lessons that you give me in dealing with the guards and prisoners alike, and I must say that I have been getting some exciting and beautiful results. I shall adhere to your advice diligently and venture on this week's journey with the idea that I, by myself, can do nothing but only the Christ in me.

My heart goes to you,
Martin

_____

May 21, 1989

My darling,

Yesterday I became depressed. And then I realized I was feeling deeply what was happening in China. I kept seeing a close-
up (as shown on TV) of a young man with blood running
down his face from having been beaten with a soldier's club.
Many soldiers have turned back, refusing to shoot the young
men in the square, and that is a wonderful thing. Now we will
see if the many more thousands, being sent in with guns and
tanks, will also have the courage, but mostly the understanding, to realize that they are individuals who can say no to
shooting into crowds of their own people—to any people,
because all people are ours—our family, our brothers and sisters.

Only as individuals can a true revolution be brought about
and that will be a bloodless revolution, only through a new
understanding of the world as spirit. The new impulse is a
start, but it has no idea, yet, of what it is moving toward. And
without that, without a knowledge of what we can be moving
toward, it can only flare up and fall back. It will fall back
temporarily because the time is coming for the new true spiritual revolution.

What has to be overcome is in each person. It is an awakening to a true sense of the spirit. No outer ideology, no outer
freedom can accomplish what has to take place in the holy
place of each person within himself. It is taking place, slowly.
It will be harder for the soldier, who has been so well trained
to be a nonperson, a non-individual. It will be very difficult
for those growing up in the slums, who are violent and angry
at a world that has deprived them of the basic needs for existence (including soul needs), and who have learned to be
emotional and unthinking. The new uprisings all over this
earth are the onset of freedom, which must come, but only
over a period of time, first in a few individual hearts, then in
more and more. Gandhi said it with his whole life, Dr. Schweitzer with his, and in a letter to a lieutenant: "Good never comes
through destruction, that we have seen in all revolutions. It is
the spirit that works. To create means evolution. All in it is
positive. Nothing is negative. It is to have reverence for life."
Rudolf Steiner said it, again and again, "An earnest, true
striving for truth, step-by-step, this alone leads to genuine

brotherliness, this is the magician which can best bring about the uniting of humanity."

And what of Christ, that great being who made the incomparable sacrifice so that man could become individual, no longer one of a mass but could stand alone as "I am!" What of his teachings of love and caring, of brotherliness? It will come. Hopefully, it will not have to take another two thousand years.

Does one truly feel what is happening around the world? I say, "Yes," whether consciously or not. Someday that will also come about—we will know more consciously what is happening to others, just as surely as today we know what is happening to the little finger on our own hand.

With love,
Ruth

———

May 26, 1989

My beautiful Ruth,

I cannot explain why, but somehow I have always known that the spiritual world is real. The church that I grew up in made a bad impression on my mind as a kid. Until I met you, I used to literally fear the spirit world because of my upbringing, and for this reason I have cursed God many times for making me afraid of Him. This is a good example of the spiritual damage that ignorant church leaders inflict on young souls. I was so deeply indoctrinated with false teachings concerning God that it was impossible for me to love Him.

There were things that used to happen to me, even until the time I met you that I still don't understand, so perhaps you can enlighten me. Sometimes when I am in a state of semi-sleepfulness, it seems like something tries to pull me farther into a deeper sleep, and for some reason, I am deathly afraid to go any deeper; when I try to become fully awake, I cannot. Then I panic and try to scream and cannot. It is like the whole physical body is immobilized, and after a minute or two of struggling, I finally become conscious again.

At the end of my first prison sentence, I had an out-of-body experience like the man in the article you sent me. I saw myself lying on my bunk. Everything seemed so peaceful, and for some reason, I kept staring at my body lying on the bunk and didn't care if I never got up again. It didn't last very long, and when I got up, I started looking around, expecting people to be staring at me in surprise and asking me what I was doing up there. Nobody was paying any attention, and when later I tried to relate this experience to some guys I thought would understand because of their high level of intelligence, they ended up making me sound like a fool. So I have kept it to myself until now. I am so happy you sent me this article. It gives me great comfort to think that you know my deepest secrets without my telling you. My heart is thumping joyously while writing this and I am smiling happily. I love you so very, very much. I thank you dearly.

I love you dearly,
Martin

————

May 29, 1989

My loving Ruth,

Last night I went to sleep, smilingly, thinking about you, and this morning I awoke, smilingly, thinking about you.

A feeling so beautiful came over me Sunday until I actually felt I could float. I was lying on the floor trying to catch what little breeze I could because it was so terribly hot. I kind of dozed off while reading, and suddenly a breeze, uncommonly light, hit me in the face; it seemed to cool not only my body but my soul as well. It was so pure and beautiful, unlike anything I had ever experienced. Upon opening my eyes, I remember thinking almost desperately that I must convey my feelings and thanks to Ruth because she is responsible for this. These humble words below, as much as I can with words, express my love and appreciation to one such as you.

To Ruth with Love
Today I give humble thanks to the good and all-seeing master.
I thank Thee for the evil storms Thou hast placed before me
    to strengthen me in spiritual body.
I thank Thee for giving me hate, for without it I could never know
    love.

I give thanks for my unforgiving accusers, for without them I should
  never know compassion.
I thank Thee for a criminal heart, for without it I would not have
  followed your directed path.
I thank Thee for my prison walls, for it is the only real church
  I have known.
I thank Thee for my false pride, for without it I could not appreciate
  humility.
I give thanks for all of these brutal and prickly thorns in my life,
  for it is only among them have I found the ineffable and
  beautiful Ruth.

Much love,
Martin

———————

May 30, 1989

Darling,

I love being called darling. So, to borrow a phrase from you,
"You can use it forever." And thanks for the beautiful poem.

The Cuban man you describe is crying out for help—the way
a child does who can be very obnoxious at times. He is away
from home. The language is unfamiliar, and he must use a
foreign tongue, in which he cannot express himself. He is
locked up in a cage, and he is alone and terrified. He is not
allowed to do anything that can ease his restless spirit. Haven't
you walked in his shoes? What was it like for you as a child?
Who heard your cries for help? Who knew the feelings that
were in your soul, that you could not express?

In Scotland I worked with handicapped children for a while.
One boy was especially difficult. He screamed a lot, particularly at night, while I tried to sleep in an alcove next to his
room. He dirtied his bed, not just wet, but mess, and got his
hands in it and smeared it all over the bed and on the walls.
I had never taken care of any children, let alone the handicapped. And now a strange thing. Life has a way of preparing
us, if we listen. We get our lessons one at a time, and each
leads to the next. I had a dog back in California, a very mixed
breed, who was quite exceptional, and she taught me how to

communicate and how to "listen," much as Strongheart in the book *Kinship With All Life*. She was wise and wonderful.

So, using her listening lessons, and praying a lot, I learned to hear the child. He was spastic. He couldn't talk. He couldn't control his walking. He couldn't swallow food very well, and it would come back up. But when I learned to "hear" him, he began to change. In one month he was a different being. He didn't always get what he wanted, but I could tell him what it was and explain why he could not have it (if that was the case) and he did not object. He only needed to be heard and to have someone say, "I hear you." He turned out to be one of the dearest, most loving beings I have ever known. He taught me a great deal. I was a child, myself, at thirty-eight.

The most important lesson for me has been how to see the world as it really is and *how* to live in it. The world is not such a nice place. It is very sick. How do we become healers in it? I think that is what you are headed for. Perhaps in our next lives we can work together? Something to look forward to.

I will try to answer your questions about the odd experiences between waking and sleeping. Every night, when we sleep, the astral body and ego (I use this to mean the higher, individual, spiritual part of us) leave the physical body and etheric (the life body) on the bed and go through certain experiences in the spirit world. They are the bodies that have consciousness, so when they are out, there is no consciousness and we are asleep. However, it sometimes happens that consciousness remains during that time and then one can look down at one's own body. The fear that comes when you are falling asleep may just be the unfamiliarity of being aware of the falling asleep process. One usually just suddenly loses consciousness. In this case, you felt your consciousness separating from the physical. Some people try to cultivate that. It is called "astral flight." There are also other names.

One should *not* try to make it happen. It can be harmful if one doesn't know what one is doing. There is a tendency in these times to plunge into such things without any idea of the preparation that is needed before going headlong into taking shortcuts into spiritual worlds. As a matter of fact, with right training we do not work at such things directly, but let them come when the spirit world finds us ready. Use prayer to ask that no harm come to you and that nothing be given to you for which you are not ready. It is especially imperative that one develop morality first, before working directly on *any* spiritual center, and also to have some idea of the pitfalls and dangers.

I'm still a bit surprised, dear one, by the way there seems to be no barrier to our understanding each other. I can't think of anyone else with whom I have this rapport. It is amazing to have found even one person who has such an open door to "listening" and exchanging ideas without prejudice or pre-conceived beliefs, or a limited area beyond where one cannot go. It is also rare to have an exchange with someone who doesn't get hurt feelings about something they think I meant, which I haven't, and who refuses to discuss it or to give up such unverified assumptions. They just jump to false con-clusions and cling to them for dear life. It reminds me of the poem "Friendship" by Craik, which I sent you, "Oh the com-fort, the inexpressible comfort, of feeling safe with a person, having neither to weigh thoughts, nor measure words."

Very, very much love,
Ruth

CHAPTER 7

Dealing with Anger

June 2, 1989

Dearest son,

Very early this morning, while awaking, old memories began
to awaken within. They had to do with anger, and they covered a very long span of time, starting very long ago. They
were not new. I had remembered parts before, at various
times. What was new was that understanding came with them
in a new way—and healing. (Someday healing will include
working with old memory and karma.)

I felt my chest begin to uncramp for the first time in probably
over a thousand years. And I seemed able to take deeper
breaths instead of the shallow breathing I have had all of this
life. And I coughed, deeply, from the depths of the lungs,
loosening up a congestion that has been there for months. The
memory, one that I believe first started a terrible anger, made
me want to scream as I had so long ago when a terrible event
had brought on a kind of insanity and almost constant screaming, while locked in a dungeon. The injury had been done,
not to me, but to my small child, the very hardest thing for a
mother to bear. As I lay in bed, remembering, I felt pain,
without pain, knew awful screaming without a sound, and
intense weeping without shedding a tear. And then love
poured forth, toward people I know and those I do not.
Though, as far as I know, you were not in the old memories,
I felt you with me, and felt how you would be the one who
would understand, and to whom I want to tell this story. But I
cannot tell it now. It is long and involved and it would be like
wrenching out part of myself, my chest and lungs and heart.

So I will tell it to you one day. The intensity of the experience, plus having had a very active day yesterday, leaves me
quite exhausted, though peaceful. I feel so close to you, and I

can feel the experience of meeting you one day as being very real. And it feels as though this memory could help to bring healing, and help me to live long enough to meet you. My chest aches this morning and that is very likely part of the healing, for healing is often accompanied by pain. It is also a story for you because it is about anger, and you will understand the kind of anger it tells about. Maybe it can also help you. I, too, went through a period of violence, in later lives, expressed by my becoming a warrior and by actually feeling good at thrusting a spear into the body of an opponent. I went through a period in this life of having great pain in just that part of my body. I think it was not the act itself, but my attitude at the time, that brought the karma connected with it.

I love you enormously,
Ruth/Mom

―――――――――

June 19, 1989

Darling Martin,

I have been trying to think, for some time, of how to tell you what you mean to me and I don't find words. I know you feel the same. I smile at the lovely things you say about me and try to tell you they are overdone. But I know how you feel. We have an openness and trust and understanding between us that is very rare and very beautiful. No words can tell you what that means to me.

There was a big, fat groundhog in the backyard today, only a few feet from the house. He seemed to sense that he was being watched through the window, and he soon stopped eating weeds and waddled off. I'll bet he was the one who ate my cucumber and bean plants last year. He left a few beans and some zucchini, but now my gardening days are over for this lifetime. I am glad Mr. Groundhog (or Mrs.) could wander about the yard without our being in competition.

How beautifully put, your saying that you feel totally safe with me. I trust you absolutely, as well.

As you think about it more, you will come to realize that not being rewarded for love makes a great deal of sense. True love has nothing of possessiveness in it. It must be free of any reward. It must be absolutely free. That's what makes it love.

One thing to be aware of is the difference between thought and deed. Sometimes we think we understand things perfectly and are shocked to discover that putting them into practice is another step we may not yet have mastered. So be very patient and loving toward yourself in the same way as you are toward others. We all have the same needs and hungers and imperfections.

Another thought about love and deeds: Eventually one thinks less of reward or punishment, but does what must be done because it is the right thing to do. We stop trying to feel important, or trying to impress people, or feeling we need to be looked up to, or any of those false values that the world teaches us. We learn not to compete but to support and help. And we do what we believe in even if the world attacks us for being different. At the same time, one need not expose one's difference unnecessarily. I'm sure you already have the following statement from Hermes. I copy it here to make sure because it is extremely important: "It is necessary to mete out truth according to individual capacities; one must veil it for the weak, whom it would drive mad, and hide it from the wicked, who can grasp only bits with which they make weapons of destruction. Seal it in your heart and let it speak in your works. Knowledge will be your strength, Faith your sword, Silence your impenetrable armor."

June 20—Darling, the heart acted up a bit during the night. Nothing serious, but it made me realize that it is important to assure you (I know that I am repeating myself) that whatever comes, whenever, it will be all right. You must be glad with and for me, but most of all know that I am with you, loving, helping, being mother, teacher, student, companion, and so on. I'm sure you will know of my presence, but if you do not at first, I will find ways to let you know. In the meantime, I am very much alive and expect to hang around for about ten years more, till the end of the century. The world will change a lot in the next ten years. A great struggle is going on between good and evil, between progress and its opposition. We will all have the opportunity to take part in it, even from where you are.

Much love always,
Ruth/Mom

June 21, 1989

My darling Ruth,

I want to tell you something about how I was committed to a mental institution. In order for it to make some sense I must start somewhere near the beginning of the story to give you an idea of the contributing factors.

Upon being released from prison, I swore I would never return, even if it meant killing and dying, and I meant it. I did not realize at the time how unprepared and ill-equipped I was to deal with the society to which I was returning. After three years of being incarcerated, I was being released with a hundred dollars, no place to stay, no job skills, and no education, which was partly my fault because the opportunities had been available. But I was just too busy building a reputation as a bad guy, which was actually justifiable at the time because the average guys my age were being raped and taken advantage of in other ways by the more seasoned convicts.

After living with my parents for about two months, I could ill afford to get a place of my own. Work was very scarce at that time of year and my mother made it emphatically clear that the sooner I got a place of my own the better. The following week I had my own apartment with thick carpet on the floor, a big air conditioner to keep the place cool, and a sawed-off shotgun to be convincing. Two months later I was the owner of two cars and more friends than I knew what to do with. Some of them were envious, some were afraid of me, but most of them were just using me and I knew it but didn't care as long as everybody seemed happy. It was then that I got involved with a character in a plot to commit a bank robbery and this led to my being taken into custody.

After witnessing my arrest on the 10:00 P.M. news, cops came from counties all around to charge me with armed robberies they felt sure I committed but couldn't prove. I think they were hoping that, with all of the pressure I had on me, I would just break down and cop out to all of their unsolved crimes. But they were all in for a big surprise. I knew that if I was convicted of some of the charges, I could be sentenced to prison for the rest of my life without parole.

Since no one could get me to talk, it was recommended that I see a psychologist. When I sat down in the comfortable chair in his office, he greeted me as though we were well-acquainted. He then proceeded to ask me if I knew what day it was, where I was, and what I was being charged with. I asked him for a cigarette as though he hadn't spoken a word. He began explaining to me about all of the various diseases that smoking can cause though he had an open pack lying on his desk.

I let him ramble on about thirty seconds, and then I stood up and suddenly dived across the desk at him. Before I could get to him, he gave the loudest scream I have ever heard; the cops, who were standing outside the door, were on me like a pack of wolves. After they got me all chained up again, I heard one of the cops whisper to the other, "I told you that S.O.B. is crazy." And that's when I started forming the idea to act insane. So while I was chained up and lying on the floor in the psychologist's office, I began to laugh at the things I was going to do, and it was really funny. My laughing only convinced the psychologist all the more that I was really insane.

In his haste to recompose himself, the psychologist told the cops that I was extremely psychotic and dangerous and that I should be committed to an insane asylum immediately, so I could be watched twenty-four hours a day. Two days later I was in a mental institution for the criminally insane.

Upon entering the big brown building at the mental institution, I suddenly got the feeling that I was in for a bizarre experience. I sort of expected the attitudes of the staff members to be somewhat similar to the guards at the prison. Man, was I in for a big surprise! All of the staff members seemed mild-mannered; the reason for this was obvious when I entered my sleeping section, which was an open dorm. All of the patients seemed to be existing in a hypnotic drug daze. They were very submissive, even when given the slightest instructions. There were guys talking to the walls, some were walking in one spot while talking to some invisible being, and some were openly staring at me as though I was an alien. There was a pool table, a Ping-Pong table, and a big television set in the day room. The staff members were just lazying around on the big comfortable chairs.

The next day I was escorted to the medical department for a checkup. The doctor told me that I seemed to be in good health. After leaving the medical department, I talked to our ward's psychologist and psychiatrist. The next day they prescribed 55 mg of Mellaril three times a day. They were giving it to me in pill form, and I would hide it under my tongue and spit it out as soon as possible.

To keep myself busy, I used to voluntarily help the staff members keep the ward clean and for this they never really insisted that I take my medication. After being there about six months, I decided to pass the test and go back to the county jail so I could get a firm understanding of my legal situation and position. Thirty days after passing the competency test I was back in the county jail.

Upon conferring with my public defender, I was told that the county was raring to prosecute me, and the best I could hope for was a life sentence. My charges were armed robbery, armed burglary, kidnapping, assault with a deadly weapon, and possession of illegal arms. He said that the state was willing to accept a guilty plea in return for a life sentence. I asked him what did he think I should do, and when he said to plead guilty, I knew then that my only hope was myself. I don't know what gave me the confidence, but I knew everything was going to work out all right. He also told me that I had charges against me pending in another county. I think the rest of the counties had given up on me for lack of evidence.

The other county's jail is the place where I discovered an anger within me so deep that the only word I can think of, in my most objective moments, to describe it, is that it is a terrifying disease. When I was being transported, the transporting officer and I were having a real good conversation. When we arrived in front of the jail, he let me out of the car and I stood there for a second or two talking to him, handcuffed behind my back.

While we were standing there talking, a jailer walked outside and yelled in a real mean voice, "Get your a—— in here before I drag you in." I immediately stepped around the other officer and told him it would take an army of punks like him before he could drag me anywhere. I proceeded walking toward the door with a swagger, and when the jailer was behind me, he tried to swing his arm around my neck. Before he could do so, I quickly backed my chin to my upper chest; this caused him to grab my face with his hands, and somehow one of his fingers slipped into my mouth and I bit down on it as hard as I could. Just when I tasted his blood, I heard him scream at the top of his lungs. Before I knew it jailers were coming from everywhere, and when they reached us, I still had this guy's finger in my mouth. They had to practically pry my mouth open before I released his finger.

After the incident, I was booked into the jailhouse and escorted to a punishment cell. They literally threw me inside and locked the door. I was then ordered to back up to the flap of the door so they could take the handcuffs off. After the handcuffs came off, they told me to take off all of my clothes and pass them out through the flap on the door. I started walking toward the bunk as though I didn't hear them. When the order came again, I sneeringly told them to come and get them, and come and get them they did! The door to the cell was so small that only one officer could come through at a time, and I immediately took advantage of this, smashing my fist into his face as many times as I could before they crowded me against the wall. By the time all of the guards got into that small cell, the fight was over and something with a sledgeham-mer impact hit me on the side of the temple; I remember everything going black. When I regained consciousness, I was naked and flat on my back and four-point chained to the metal bunk. They refused to give me medical treatment, even though I was bleeding from a head wound.

My public defender was told that I was too violent to be allowed out of the cell to confer with him, therefore he had to come to me. He told me that the only charges they could make a case out of against me in court were two counts of dealing in stolen property. I laughed scornfully and told him that was impossible because dealing in stolen property wasn't my style. Unfortunately, the state had two witnesses against me—two witnesses that knew me quite well. Both witnesses had come to me for favors in the past, and they were not turned down. Upon hearing their names coming out of the public defender's mouth, a rage so black and strong swelled within me until I thought that I was going to be suffocated by my anger. The public defender, after realizing that I wasn't going to talk any more, finally left.

Somehow the county judge heard that I was being chained to my bunk day and night, and he advised them of the illegality of chaining me to the bunk for too long and ordered them to release me. Before they released me, a sergeant at the jail came into the cell with two other jailers. The sergeant placed his left foot on my neck and told me, "The only reason you aren't dead is because we don't have a place to bury your black a——.

Now do you think you have learned how to be a good nigger?"
I turned my head as much as I could so that I could look him
in the face and gave a guttural sound to let him know that he
was choking me. When he took his foot from my neck, I spit
in his face. He leaned against the top bunk to support his
weight while he lifted his right foot and began kicking me in
the head. The old wound that had closed by itself opened up
again. The moment he started kicking me, I kept spitting as
though I was possessed. My spitting only enraged him all the
more, and he started kicking me with more force and suc-
cession as though he was in a hypnotic state.

I guess somewhere deep in my soul I had decided that I was
just tired of life, people, and the lying and treacherous games
that people play. I thought of how I never remembered my
parents, or anyone, taking me in their arms and saying, "I
love you," or uttering other endearments that one's soul needs
to hear sometimes to warm their hearts.

Alas, I was truly a living corpse, and it is no longer a wonder
that I was unconsciously looking for someone to bury me. And
this guy would have done it for me if one of his subordinate
officers hadn't stopped him after noticing that I had passed
out and was bleeding profusely from the head, mouth, and
nose. The nurse and other medical staff were summoned, and
when they could not bring me to, I was immediately rushed
to the nearest hospital. That's where I was when I next opened
my eyes. The story they gave for my being in that shape was
that when they came to release me from the bunk, as ordered
by the judge, as soon as they released me I started fighting
like a maniac and my physical condition was the end result.

All of the officers' stories correlated with each other. I did
not contest their lies, and they openly showed their surprise.
I looked at each one from my hospital bed and started laughing
at their naked fear, and I think from that day on each of them
had a certain fear of me because they realized that I did not
value my life as they did theirs. As soon as I was released
from the hospital, they had it arranged to send me back to the
mental institution.

To be continued

My darling Ruth, I want you to know that it is doing my soul
a lot of good for me to be emotionally able to narrate these

past events to you. You are the first soul that I am able to communicate with, as I am doing, without feeling shame or embarrassment. For this you have relieved me of great burdens untold. I shall always stand before you humbly and without shame.

It's now mail pick-up time.

To Mom, I send you everlasting love,
Martin

———

June 26, 1989

Darling Ruth,

To continue: When I was released from the hospital, I was taken back to the punishment cell to wait for my transfer back to the mental institution. The second day out of the hospital, the head nurse came to my cell with two of the guards trailing in her footsteps. She handed me a small medicine cup with a liquid and told me to drink it. I asked her what was it, and she said it was something the doctor ordered for me to get well. I knew then that it wasn't anything to do me any good, so I told her I didn't want it. She said I could either take it or they would come in and inject it into me by force. I took it, and she made sure I swallowed it by making me open my mouth and stick out my tongue.

A couple of minutes later my vision started blurring and I couldn't control my body's equilibrium, so I had to lay my body on the small bunk to keep from falling. All I could do was stare at the ceiling. It took all the energy I had to keep myself from going to sleep, and finally I had to submit because the medication was too much. I think their plan was to keep my physically restrained by whatever means available, and since they couldn't legally keep me chained to the bunk any-more, they decided to keep me medicated. Seemingly there was nothing I could do about it, because they had convinced my family that I had lost my mind completely, and when my mother came to visit me one Sunday afternoon, she did not find it strange at all that all I could do was stare at her through the little glass window in my door while lying on my bunk.

Before she left, I remember her saying that she was going to pray for me.

The guards used to come by and make fun of me every chance they could, because all I could do was sleep and stare at things while trying to maintain a little sanity within the deep recesses of my mind. I remember waking up one morning for breakfast and thinking I was in a restaurant. In my drug-induced hallucination, Superman was sitting in front of me in the restaurant and we were conspiring to break me out of jail at 12:00 noon. After conspiring with Superman, the thought of breaking out gave me enough energy to wash myself as best I could in the sink. After accomplishing this great feat, I then sat down on my bunk awaiting the arrival of my accomplice. I kept inquiring of the guards about the time every thirty minutes, and when one finally asked me if I was going somewhere, I almost panicked. So to keep them from getting suspicious, I lay back on my bunk and before I knew it I was asleep.

Within the deep recesses of my sleep, I heard a faraway banging—it was getting louder and louder. I was thinking it must be Superman, and in my excitement I jumped out of my bunk and yelled at the top of my voice, "Superman, Superman, I'm in here!" I started looking around inside my cell expecting him to come through the ceiling or the wall, and it finally dawned on me that the guards were banging on the cell door telling me to get ready to leave; they were laughing like crazy. Listening to them laugh at me like that made me want to crawl right out of life. At that time, it seemed to me that they had finally succeeded in stripping me of the only thing I had left— my pride. So I sat down on my bunk and cried until they ordered me to come to the flap to be handcuffed. I passively obeyed.

Being committed to the mental institution a second time was accepted with an eagerness—I needed to get there to recuperate from the beating I had suffered and to salvage what little pride I had left. Upon entering the hospital again, the first thing I learned was that the patients could no longer be forced to take the medications that were being heaped upon them by the staff members. What a blessing! This gave me a chance to "dry out" from the very large doses they forced me to take at the county jail.

For a whole week all I did was lie in the big hospital bed

and go back and forth to the chow hall, while collecting my thoughts and trying to figure out my legal advantages, if, in fact, I had any. A week later I started going to the library, but the few legal books they had didn't have any information pertaining to my case.

After the pain from the beating I had suffered in the county jail had nearly ceased agonizing me, I started helping the staff keep the ward clean again, and eventually, I was doing all the cleaning. I didn't mind because it kept me busy and made me feel a lot closer to my environment.

A month later I was again a Ping-Pong celebrity. I took extra pleasure in beating the staff members because they used to beat us patients at all of the softball games. The biggest reason for this was because most of the patients were on medication. After being on the medication for a long period of time, the guys couldn't seem to do without it. From observing other guys taking medicines and after consuming it for a period in the county jail, it seemed to me that the medication took away any inclination and will to make one's own decisions. It also had a terrible effect on the nervous system.

Everything began to be a predictable routine at the hospital. I passed my next competency test, so I could get back to the county jail to do some legal research on my case.

Since being arrested, I realized that up until now I had been intentionally avoiding thinking about why my partner had set the job up and then deserted me. I had blocked him out of my mind to keep from going insane because I used to get killing mad whenever his face or name entered my mind. I knew I had been set up, and it was killing me inside not knowing why, with my friend on the streets patting himself on the back for a job well done. And what was upsetting me more than anything was that this guy seemed to be confident that I wouldn't rat him out to the cops, and he was right. The only comfortable thoughts that I could entertain toward him were fantasizing about the many ways to torture him before I killed him.

The six months that I spent in the mental institution the second time had somewhat rejuvenated me. Then I was returned to the jail. Two months later I met my lying accusers at my first disposition hearing. This was only a hearing to give the state a chance to show cause, or enough evidence, to continue with trial proceedings. After hearing my friends give their fabricated and inconsistent testimonies against me, I was rather sure that the state would drop the ridiculous charges against me. But it was not to be. They were just as persistent in convicting me as I was in maintaining my innocence.

I exercised more control than I had originally anticipated during the hearing. A calm realization dawned on me that my friends were only pawns in a game to be used against me. Perhaps they were not lying out of hatred and animosity, but rather to save their own necks. I have always wondered if I were in their shoes, would I have done the same thing to someone else. During the trial, my public defender assured me that we were going to win the case. Two months later we lost it, and the judge gave me nine years in the state prison for dealing in stolen property. My public defender looked at me and shrugged his shoulders as though we had only flipped a coin and lost.

Much love,
Martin

———————

June 26, 1989
My darling,

I relive the experiences you describe of your battles with the guards. I see it over and over in my mind and something emerges. It is as if you have two choices, either submissiveness or fight, and on both sides plenty of anger. They are clever, the invisible evil ones, they who get us to fight one another, to hate one another. In a recent letter you said you were learning how to drop the tough-guy image without surrendering your dignity along with it. And that, of course, is a third way. It is a quality of soul. It must be how Christ carried himself on the walk up the hill to Golgotha and how he was, even on the cross. It is choosing who, what, and how you will be no matter what is out in the world. It is dignity, but not pride, humility without self-effacement, love without desire, love which has no reward.

Thank you for being you, for being my friend, for writing to me and letting me write to you, for loving me and letting me love you. You are beautiful.

Here is the story of my anger. It is difficult to write, but I think it may be good for you to hear it, so I'll try: It is hard to find the words to describe it, for it tells something about the world that is unpleasant to hear. It was very long ago. My vision is of a huge mass of people who have gathered for a rite—to celebrate the dedication of a new temple. The dedication consists of several people being buried alive in a large pit dug beneath the new building. The head person, a terrible ruler, is, of course, having his enemies—those who oppose him and his evil ways—put into the pit. I am also an enemy, but he has pretended to be friendly. I have been forced to be there, and I am holding my baby in my arms. I do not realize that I have been surrounded by his henchmen, and at the last minute, just before a top is put on the pit and it is covered, they tear the baby from my arms and hold me back, fighting and screaming, while the baby is put into the pit with the others. Such intense feelings still rise up in me so that I can find no words to describe it—the submissive, cheering mob, the awful feeling of the evil of that place, the disgust I feel for the inhumanity of the people and the horror of my child in that pit. I am dragged off to the dungeon, screaming and quite out of my mind.

Although my memory is unclear after that, it seems I eventually died in that dungeon. The leader (priest I'm sure) had always pretended to be a friend, though I had opposed his manipulations, tricks, lies, and mistreatment of others. I have the impression that he wanted me and had hoped to win me to his ways. When he knew that would not happen, he did the worst possible thing that one can do to a mother. I had been naive and had not realized the extent of evil in people, especially him. I seem to have remained naive in this regard over many lifetimes. I have had to deal with evil a thousand times, in a thousand ways, and perhaps I have finally learned a bit about it—mostly that people choose it. This was the unbelievable aspect that was so difficult for me to grasp. I had to be betrayed and tortured and executed innumerable times before it became clear to me that that is normal behavior for many people.

The result of that experience was a terrible anger, and also sadness, which carried through a number of lifetimes. There is a memory of one incident, of the satisfaction of forcefully thrusting a spear into an opponent, while fighting in a war.

Becoming a warrior may have been a way that some of that anger could be spent. I know of one other memory of being a man. At about the age of nineteen, I see myself walking way out to sea to commit suicide. The earth there slopes gently, and it is a very long walk to where the sea covers my head and I drown. It is done slowly with unquestioned determination. It is because of terrible unhappiness at the people, their selfishness, greed, hatred, self-chosen ignorance and corruption. That may have been in Greece. I have a number of memories of having been executed, not for being bad, but for fighting evil. And the worst of all were the very people one was fighting for. How well I understand your poem—"when it is only for them that I shed these tears."

I am sure I came to the earth sphere very long ago—an alien—to try to work here as a kind of missionary, coming to an evil, a backward place, and I keep coming back, still trying. To fight evil one has to understand evil. Over and over again I was overcome because I could not believe such cruelty would be deliberately chosen. This earth is not really a nice place. The task now is to understand how degraded it can be and yet to keep trying. It is a particularly evil time. That is not hard to see. And there is much ignorance, hatred, greed, corruption, violence. To start with, one must clear all these things from oneself, for as residents of earth we are also contaminated with the diseases of earth. And then we need to find the true spirit within, and through that, to build up love and caring and courage. Because the evil ones are proficient liars, we have to learn how to recognize them despite how they appear from the outside. And we must learn trust and hope in the spirit world, in those good spirit beings who work with us if we will only work with them. But we must learn to *know* the enemy— a difficult thing when he pretends to be our friend and is very clever at it.

It is not easy to understand evil, partly because, to people who are intent on doing the best that we can, it seems unbelievable. There is also the consideration that there is a difference between evil people and those who do evil things because of ignorance. The evil ones deliberately cultivate it, make evil choices intentionally. It may be for the ignorant that we fight until they can make their own choice. C. S. Lewis seems to have an understanding of evil, and I hope you will have an opportunity to read his *Space Trilogy*, which is included in the list of recommended books I sent you recently. Let me know if the library is able to get them for you.

I hadn't expected a paper on anger to lead to material on evil, but I guess they do go hand-in-hand. I will be very interested in your thoughts regarding it.

I send you love always,
Ruth

June 28, 1989

My darling Ruth,

Ahh, my love, you are a wonderfully brave one, and your kind of courage makes me love you all the more, if such a thing is possible. I know that physical death for us all is inevitable, and since becoming aware of the afterlife, I am forever trying to cultivate the strength to deal with it as you are. So if you should pass away before me, I promise that I shall try with all I have to be happy with you and for you. I must also tell you that I know there is nothing that can separate us now. I love you so very much. And if you go before me, I promise you that I will always be receptive to your visits, love, help, and so on.

After contemplating the idea that "love must be free of any reward," it has joyfully occurred to me that this is the only kind of love that is beyond the reach of mortality, and in order to maintain its status of immortality, it must be free of all expectations. Not being rewarded for love makes a whole lot of sense, thank you.

I am very glad that you pointed out the difference between the thought and the deed. I am discovering every day that there is a vast difference and that the two must become one to be totally successful.

To Mom with love,
Martin

July 4, 1989

My dearest Ruth,

How well you seem to know my thoughts sometimes. Yes, I was beginning to believe, before meeting you, that the only forces in the world were insanity and violence and terror. These are the forces that were beginning to shape my constitution. I think a lot of people fall prey to these forces if they are not rescued like I was.

I am using your beautiful words as a form of meditation: "It is dignity, but not pride, humility without self-effacement, love without desire, love which has no reward." I thank you for giving them to me.

I have your old pastels and watercolor paintings that you have been sending me laid out all over my cell while writing this letter. They are all a great treat. That they are on 9×12 paper makes it possible for me to have them, and I so appreciate your sending them to me. Thank you.

Lately I have been scrutinizing my anger in an effort to ascertain why I react to certain situations with violence and hostility. It is a fact that most prisoners' attitudes and dispositions are molded by their prison environment. In most cases one's survival depends on what his fellow prisoners may think of him. In view of these facts, my attitude and disposition have been shaped by my environment. Abiding by the hardcore prisoner code of conduct has been my way for a long time. And now it is time for a change, and I welcome it with my whole being.

Much love,
Martin

———

July 8, 1989

Darling,

On Thursday evening a couple stopped here to look at the house, and by the next afternoon (just yesterday) we had signed the agreement. Now we only need to wait for all the procedures to go through—the loan from the bank, the title check, and so on. After six years, from when I first began trying to sell it, with almost no interest in it at all, suddenly in one day it has happened. I am in shock. All I can feel is panic about all that needs to be done. There will be help from angels and people, and I really know all will be fine, but a part of me still insists on panic. We set a date of August 25th for me to be gone.

I suppose you realize we are approaching our first anniversary of your first letter dated August 8, 1988. How shall we celebrate? I will try to send something special, and maybe light a candle and have a special prayer of thanks along with a wish for an early release and a meeting for us. It doesn't hurt to ask.

Here is a quote from you, " . . . the magic, love, joy, and beauty that you are maturing within me." No, my dearest Martin, *you* are maturing within yourself! I am showing, you are doing. It is all within you and you are bringing it forth.

One thought on my mind, lately, has been about how hard it is to see injustice without reacting strongly. Writing my anger story to you has helped me, and I now take on the task of learning to observe injustice with equanimity.

It is very likely that you have had some experiences to match mine. I now see, that in the time I spoke of, when you were my son, we were all murdered by a horde of marauding invaders sweeping across the country, raiding just for the heck of it. We were four—husband, wife, you, and a younger, very gentle, frail sister. You seem to have been about ten, and the expression I see on your face is surprise and disbelief at such behavior. I imagine you still have that. It is important for you to realize, as it has been for me, that it is a fact of life on this earth. There are such people and they are all about us. And they do not always express in physical violence. And they can have a very pleasant outer exterior. Once you accept the idea, you eventually can learn to recognize them. It is good to recognize the evil that is in this world, to see it for what it is, and to learn to know how it works.

I heard about your upcoming trial from another prisoner we correspond with. I suppose you did not say anything in order to be protective of me. But it is good for us both that I know, for then I can be with you in spirit. Can you tell me just what will take place? All he said was that you seem to accept "what will be."

You are so easy to love and I love you much,
Ruth

CHAPTER 8

Freedom in Bondage

July 17, 1989

Darling,

Because of you today has been a most beautiful day. It is because you have given me the love, wisdom, and understanding to take notice of the things one usually overlooks and takes for granted. God's creation is everywhere at all times, therefore so is beauty. There are times, when I am looking through my bars, that I experience a freedom that few have experienced anywhere, and something tells me that this is a freedom that cannot be taken away but must be rightfully earned.

Thank you for the Prayer of St. Francis of Assisi. It is truly a divine work.

I don't remember exactly what ages I started going through changes in my childhood. I do remember trusting and loving everything and everyone at a real young age. I can also remember thinking that people were just naturally friendly toward each other and that everyone in the world had everyone's best interest at heart. I woke up one morning and all of this was gone.

Dearest, I believe it is important to let you know that you are the fuel that maintains what little light I have, and that is abundant compared to what I had. I thank you for reaching out. I do not find one soul in this environment who can discuss anything beyond the conventional and the surface teachings. There is only prejudice and blind stubbornness, therefore you are my only source of real information and learnings.

Yes, the guards can see everything inside my cell. The only remarks from them are that I keep a neat cell. Even though it is against policy to keep pictures on the wall, they haven't said anything about it. They are hanging by sewing thread, so they can be taken down without damaging them.

Your letters make me "think, think, think." I am very grateful and blessed by your love and teachings.

Much love,
Martin

July 20, 1989

Darling Martin,

Things are going much better than I expected because friends are helping.

Diane has a train ticket for the 18th of August, arriving on the 20th. We'll probably leave here in my car about the 24th and go to Memphis to visit my dear friends there, who are like family, and then start home. It will be early September when we arrive in California.

Much, much love,
Ruth

July 26, 1989

My darling Ruth,

I am very happy to hear that you have plenty of help. I can imagine how difficult it is trying to get things done in a wheelchair.

I have a court hearing scheduled for July 31 at 9:00 A.M. My public defender has filed a motion to withdraw from my case because I have refused to talk to him.

I am thinking of the people who came to help you move. I love the converging of dear people, especially with children around to make the reunion complete. Children seem to have a beautiful spiritual aura that most grownups lack. When I was going to grade school in the northern states, people were people, blacks and whites going to school together, seemingly without any problems. The atmosphere was very relaxed, and I remember the grades on my report cards were so excellent that my parents bought me some new clothing to go to school in. One of my uncles was even setting aside money for a college fund for me.

The farther we moved down south, the faster I grew up. One day I looked in the mirror and I was suddenly aware of my skin color, even though I was not fully conscious of what it symbolized to people in general, especially there in the south. The psychological race game that the world plays is very detrimental to all people. This disease is so deeply imbedded in some people's consciousness that they are not aware of it until they are suddenly faced with a situation that forces it to surface. This disease is the author of much conceit and deceit. It is the father of the superior and inferior race complex, and I speak from experience.

In spite of the rehabilitative front that is shown to the public by prison officials, the prisons in this state are a business corporation, and the idea is to recruit rather than rehabilitate and release. With as many prison structures as we have here, we also have one of the highest overcrowding situations and return rates in the nation, and we are still building more prisons.

I do hope you enjoy your trip.

To Mom, with love,
Martin

———————

July 28, 1989

Darling Martin,

There is something to tell you. During this time of planning to go west, I had the crazy idea of flying out to see you before the drive. I even talked to Diane and she would have gone with me. But I realized as the days went by, and I was feeling so exhausted and weak, that my body would not be very cooperative. The drive will be all that I dare plan on. It was an idea I had great difficulty giving up and I cry about it now and then. What a crybaby I am! So now you will have to come to me. In the meantime, we have our letters and meeting in sleep, and our good, warm love.

I would so like to get you started on an education. Now that there is a little money from the house, if it is not too expensive, perhaps you could start a correspondence course. You must let me know if you really wish it, for I would never want to push you into anything you may not want. If you do, it would give me pleasure to help. It could be my anniversary present to you, and yours to me could be your acceptance.

Lots of love,
Ruth

————————

August 1, 1989

Dearest Ruth,

I just got back from court yesterday and my thoughts and impressions of yesterday's happenings are still in a jumble. Nothing happened except that the judge denied my public defender's motion to withdraw from my case, which did not surprise me.

After being among outside people again, I was more consciously aware than ever before that most people will quickly react to one's outer appearance only, and very few will ever take the time to look at one's inner being. From what I could observe, everyone seemed to be constantly on the move and not really going anywhere. People seemed to be so involved with themselves that they gave little or no attention to the welfare of others. It was like walking among people and really seeing them for the first time. Ignorance gives people all the rights they need to live in fear of each other.

Your letters of July 15 and July 24 arrived Friday. Enclosed were the geometric drawings, stamps, and your beautiful and inspiring poems. These are all special works of art, especially the poems. I sincerely hope that you carry the poems further, putting them in book form as you intended, for the sake of sharing them with others.

On July 27 I sent a letter to you discussing personal experiences with racism, and your letter with the law center material and your poems arrived the next day. Again our thoughts coincide.

In 1981 I walked into an all-white public establishment in the south, and because I was ignorant of the newer and upcoming hate groups, I did not recognize the racist symbols and signs that were decorating the walls of the restaurant. Needless to say my ignorance almost cost me my life. Four guys followed me out of the restaurant and started shooting at me after I was a distance away. Had I not been carrying a pistol of my own, I fear we would not be writing each other today. That incident is one of my most profound reasons for having an interest in keeping up with all of this world's hate groups. I dearly thank you for your consideration in sharing with me whatever worldly knowledge that you deem fitting and necessary.

Love yah,
Martin

August 2, 1989

My darling Ruth,

I am just ecstatic about your darling, beautiful, and crazy idea of flying out to see me before your long drive back to California. And I give special thanks to the blessed angels for dissuading you because the prison officials at this institution would not have permitted you to see me. Perhaps they would have told you it is because you are not of my immediate family or that you are not on my visiting list. They have been known to make exceptions in both cases but only when the two parties are of the same race.

I became superconsciously aware of my color between the ages of fourteen and sixteen; I'm not exactly sure when. What I am sure of is that when this awareness dawned on me, I suddenly lost interest in a lot of things. It was as though life was saying because of your skin color you cannot achieve and hope for certain things. I am sure that this is when the psychological blocks and inferiority complex began to develop from within. I am also sure that this is when my rebellious and criminal nature began. I am now going to reveal to you my discovery of the most damaging and contributing factors to this process of inferiority.

The first one, that I quickly became aware of, was our educational system. The second was all of our world's organized religions. And the most amazing one of all is that I have seen traces of this syndrome in every black person that I have ever encountered, even black professionals. What more harm can a system do to a man than to make him totally and inwardly dissatisfied with himself and wish to become as others are. This is a system, which still exists today, that was designed a long time ago for the purpose of enslaving one physically and mentally, and it has proven to be most successful even unto this day. Obviously the ancient slave masters realized that to capture a man it was not sufficient to enslave his body; it was also necessary to enlist his reason. Unfortunately, I still suffer from some of the long-term effects that the system inflicts upon one's growth, but yet I am more fortunate than most, because true awareness has finally dawned and I have begun the task of liberating myself fully. Only with you am I able to truly express myself, and I am positive that you are giving me back something that was taken away a long time ago. With you I am free to do, to think, to say, to love without fear and shame. My soul cries out with joy and happiness and thanks, and appreciation of your presence in my life and cosmic existence. Sometimes I love you so very much that I can even love the evil ones, and I think without you I would just give up. You are my source of strength, love, and inspiration.

I thank you for being my mother, teacher, friend, and especially for loving me.

To Mom with love,
Martin

―――――――

August 7, 1989

My darling Martin,

I would not have come to see you without a permit already in my hand and had, in fact, written to find out what was required. But then I realized it would not be possible. What I didn't look at, because of naiveté, was the danger to you of being visited by a white lady.

Tomorrow is our anniversary. I am thinking that just a year ago you were reading my book before writing to me. You are very important to me and I thank whoever in the spirit realm arranged our meeting.

I turned on the TV a little while ago and a young black man

was playing flute with an orchestra—classical music on public television. He was more beautiful and his music sweeter because of knowing you.

I appreciate the things you tell me of your past and understand why it was difficult for you to write about it when I suggested you try your hand at writing. I find it difficult just to read it. I hope that between us we can overcome the nonsense things imposed by a sick world and that you will one day be able to help others do it, too.

I love you much,
Ruth/Mom

August 8, 1989

My darling Ruth,

Today is a new day and it is approximately 5:30 in the morning. Happy anniversary, my dearest. From the beginning you have captured the part of me that no one else, including myself, could subdue. It was the part of me that seemed to be the most distrustful because of its vulnerability. And now, from that vulnerability, do I begin to build the rack of my strength. But for the grace of your compassionate soul I should never know love without desire, humility without surrender, dignity and not pride. I am forever grateful to whatever fate has infinitely bound our path.

I am definitely interested in advancing my education and am investigating the possibilities. I will share it with you as soon as I get a response. I'm really excited about the idea of getting schooling. It means a new and more positive start in a new direction, especially with you by my side.

Your idea of using your first name out of respect for the woman who bore me is wow, so very thoughtfully beautiful! It's the little things like this that make me love you so dearly. I am greatly blessed to have you as a mother and a friend.

Love to Ruth/Mom
Martin

August 15, 1989

My darling,

I went to another court hearing Monday. It was only on another motion that my public defender filed requesting the judge to order a psychological evaluation on my behalf before continuing trial proceedings. After he gave the judge a brief and oral review of my psychological history, the court quickly granted the motion. The evaluation will be for the purpose of determining whether or not I am competent enough to stand trial and to determine whether or not I was sane or insane at the time of the crime. Depending on the outcome of the evaluation, my address could be changing again, but we'll just wait and see what tomorrow will bring.

It's amazing the games people play when they cannot find a ready solution to their idea of what should or should not be. Alas, I must also include myself because I have been pushing the court in this direction. I think, out of the court system, you and I are the only ones who have my best interest at heart. I honestly wish I would have more faith in our judicial system, but experience has stripped me of whatever faith I might have had in it.

I recently discovered that the things they have me charged with carry a maximum penalty of fifteen years, not five as I previously thought. Even so I am confident that things will turn out for the best, whatever the results may be, because, as you so wisely advised, I am always looking to gain more understanding from whatever situation that may present itself.

I hope and pray every night that you and Diane will have a happy and safe trip back home.

Love and blessings to Ruth/Mom
Martin

August 18, 1989

Dearest Martin,

I suppose that remaining calm in the face of adversity would mean that one was really "awake in the spirit," and really knew how cared for we are. That does not mean things are "going our way," but that we have trust that whatever comes belongs to us.

How well I understand your fear/anger when having to deal with cruelty, unfairness, and deliberate manipulation. I once worked for someone who got a great kick out of stirring up trouble between his employees and getting them to attack each other verbally in front of a group. Needless to say, I didn't stay there. It took me a little while to see it because one doesn't expect it, and I didn't until he tried it on me. Yech! I simply refused to talk.

About people professing one thing and doing another, there was once a picture in a San Francisco newspaper of a young lady hitting a policeman with her peace sign. But we need to know how difficult it is to be truly true to our ideals and to watch ourselves most carefully. History is full of destruction, cruelty, greed, ignorance. But there is also heroism, great deeds, great individuals. There will be more. Greatness can and does take place in small ways. When getting along and harmonizing with people seems impossible, then we must let it go and do our best not to be like them, but to remain loving, caring. We must not let them change us. Do not think I can accomplish it yet. It is also, for me, something at which to work.

I have been picturing you in court and wondering why it is so scary to be in such a position. The thought that comes to me is that one is in a life-death situation (in a sense), and one is being judged by people with power without justice. I wonder if it helps to know that the real judge, in the end, is God. Unless we know karma, we do not know much. Unless we can see the real purpose behind things, we cannot know what it means or what we are being trained for. It is not only the victim we need to have compassion for, but the one who is, in your words, "forever scheming and setting up all kinds of wicked traps for others," for he is setting up some traps and hardships for himself.

What makes such people behave in such a way? It certainly is lack of sensitivity, like maybe something is missing inside them. I am sure, for one thing, that they are unable to love. Maybe they have never known love, have never been loved, and therefore do not know it. I shall try to make it an exercise for myself to look upon those most gross, not so much to be criticized, as to be seen to be in need of love. Maybe in another thousand years I will have learned to do it.

Love everlasting,
Ruth

August 28, 1989

My darling Martin,

We are at our first stop, my friends in Tennessee, and they are very good to us. They have taken Diane into their hearts and she them. The car is fixed after some problems with the air conditioner, which we will need in the desert, and it is gassed and oiled and we shall have a good trip. We will take our time and enjoy, and carry you in our hearts.

I love you dearly, my son,
Ruth/Mom

August 29, 1989, Arkansas

My darling,

Air conditioner trouble has sent us to a garage again for the second time, and we've gone three hundred miles in two days. Diane asks, "Are we having fun yet?" We are laughing a lot, because what else can one do? We are taking it in stride — small strides.

It is night. I'm doing my usual, falling asleep early and waking in the night. The bathroom light is on and Diane assures me it does not keep her awake, while it gives me dim light to write by. I am reading my collection of meditations, poems, sayings, and thinking of you. I found this one for you:

Evening Prayer
Thou angel of God
Who hast charge of me
From the shepherding King
Of the Spirits, of the Saints,
Make round about me this night
A protecting shield.

Be thou a bright flame before me
Be thou a smooth path below me
Be thou a guiding star above me
And be a kindly shepherd behind me
Today, tonight and forever.

I am tired and I am a stranger
Lead thou me to the land of Angels.
For me it is time to go home
To the love of Christ
To the peace of heaven.

I love you,
Ruth/Mom

September 5, 1989

Dearest Martin,

We arrived early this afternoon. We did stop at the prison on the way, and my prisoner friend and I had a four-hour visit. We spent the time in the large outdoor visiting area, a quite pleasant place, with shaded tables and benches. I felt much more relaxed than before, even though when I entered, the prison atmosphere was pretty strange again. But I just turned it off and had a good visit.

Tom is on a business trip for a few days and Ellen was at work, so there was no one here. I had expected to flop into bed and rest but suddenly got wide awake and energetic and did a bit of arranging of the furniture in my room and a little work in the house. They had had company and so I took sheets and towels and put them in the washing machine and straightened the kitchen. When Ellen came, we had to talk, of course, and then she took me out to dinner. Now I am settled in bed and can write a few letters. Tomorrow I will rest, I think. The intensity of work over the last two months and the many decisions, and then the trip, will all show their effects and I'll need to spend a little time recuperating.

Love, my dear Martin,
Ruth

September 7, 1989

My dearest Ruth,

I thank you sincerely for the beautiful meditations, sayings, and poems that you have sent lately. They are indeed spiritually uplifting.

The librarian isn't being very helpful. As a matter of fact, he has accused me of not returning the first book that I received from the interlibrary loan system. I am also being accused of not returning another book that I never received. I am not sure if this is a mistake on their part or a plot to frustrate my efforts to obtain books. The one librarian insists I have not returned the book, the other does not respond to my request forms.

About a month or so before meeting you I had come to the conclusion that something was very wrong with my life. I couldn't put my finger on it because my way of living was all I knew. Like anyone else, I was living by the standards and dictates of my environment, and suddenly I started feeling guilty about a lot of things that didn't bug me at one time, or so I thought.

One night about midnight I was looking out of my window into the darkness thinking of all the years, months, and days gone by and suddenly I felt really empty inside. I wanted to cry and I realized there were no tears within me—this realization intensified my misery. It did not stem from being in prison or lack of material gain, but from something else and at that time I knew not what. From that point, for the next two weeks, I would pray in earnest every night for whatever it was I needed to fill the void that existed within me. As I was about to lose patience, the wonderful angels brought you into my life. I know that you are the answer to my prayers because, since meeting you, the void is being filled and the misery has almost ceased to exist. Now perhaps you can better understand my great appreciation and love for you.

I received an answer about obtaining a G.E.D. It was mostly double-talk, and it seems obvious that my every effort is censored and restricted to nil by the authorities and their helpers.

To Ruth/Mom with love,
Martin

September 10, 1989

Martin dear,

I awoke this morning dreaming a strange dream about someone wrongfully jailed and simply kept there. It set me thinking.
People with money are not kept in jail. They have money and
influence. I have very little, and I have been offering you some
for schooling, but how much would it take to get you a lawyer?
It is probably way beyond my means, but how can one find
out? Why not ask questions? What can you find out for us? I
hear of special lawyer groups who take on some cases for
smaller fees.

My room is getting arranged with the help of Ellen and Tom.
Some careful planning has made it possible to put in my desk,
copier, chest of drawers (donated by one of their friends), and
plenty of book shelves, and there is a really large closet. It
will be almost a cell, but larger and well-filled with things,
mostly work things, and a few art things on the wall, and
books.

Last night I was so tired I thought I would never have
enough strength to get out of bed ever again. I little while ago
(in the middle of the night) I awoke feeling peaceful, glad to
be here, glad to have you in my heart, glad to be rereading
your letters, happy to have you to write to, feeling love overflowing to you.

It is indeed disappointing about your difficulty in getting
schooling. One can only keep trying. I do want to help if you
can arrange to do it by correspondence. I know it is difficult
for you to be so much on the receiving end, and you constantly
tell me you get by. Please read the Gibran again about giving
and receiving. And remember that I am your mother.

I love the drawings on your envelopes, especially the
house.

In your letter of August 15 you write about the relationship
between the natural world and the spiritual world. I'll try
to answer. First of all, they are not separate. Everything is
permeated with spirit. At one time man had spiritual consciousness. We lived in tune with the spiritual world. But
in order to develop consciousness of the material world, the
spiritual consciousness was dimmed. This was part of the
course of evolution. In the process, a great many people went
so far with materialism that they lost sight of the spirit alto-

gether, and they refused to acknowledge the possibility that the spirit exists. If they cannot physically touch it, weigh it, and measure it, they refuse to consider it. Real thinking would show them otherwise, for there is much we can understand through good common sense.

Now, there are also some who do not see realistically and have all sorts of odd notions about it. Many look to the past for spiritual knowledge, and though we have much to learn from it, the past belongs to the past. Evolution has brought some important changes and so what the present and future hold for us is something different. We are not supposed to give up intellectual consciousness and go back to the past, but awaken and develop new spiritual organs, which will add to the ability to perceive both worlds more clearly. There has to come a kind of "marriage" between the two.

These are not enlightened times, but the darkest of times. The deceit and greed, the cruelty and corruption we have spoken of are the result of the spiritual blindness that is so prevalent. Besides this, there are actual evil beings (as there are angels) who would mislead people away from proper development/evolution. On the positive side, this awakens us to more consciousness, and that is what should be happening during this time. Pain is a great awakener, especially soul pain. Your own experience will show you that. You spoke of your desperate feeling of emptiness and misery and your prayer for help. That is what the world is coming to, and it will happen more and more.

It is not what people tell you that is important, but what you can understand within yourself. Then you really know. What people tell you can be indications for you to work with, to help to awaken. Life, itself, helps. Just what we need at any time is right at hand if we only begin to recognize it. It can only happen because there are spiritual beings—there is a whole spiritual world—looking after us and caring. There is opposition, too, and temptation. And that comes from beings, too, evil ones. You have seen them at work, even when they are invisible. A good way to give them full rein is to refuse to see them or their works. They are having their way at the moment, quite powerfully, but that will change, gradually, as people become more awake to it and take things into their own hands. We are given indications by the spirit world, but that is all it is; the real work depends on people. That is our task on earth. It is helpful to draw back and see the picture from a less personal point of view. Then the daily annoyances and irritations at people's behavior may be easier to bear. Mostly they behave the way they do, not to be annoying to others, but because they are in a kind of sleep state. They are too unaware to do it consciously.

I want to remind you not to expect smooth sledding. We tend to think that progress is a steady upward road. Not so. There will be plenty of times when it seems impossible to cope, but it is in overcoming that we grow. It is helpful to have a goal in mind and to hold on to it when everything seems hopeless. Talk to me then, whether I am on earth or in spirit realms. The love between us will always be there.

If you find me repeating some things, it could be forgetfulness on my part, but it could also be intentional because we do not learn without hearing things over and over. This I found especially true in teaching handwork, and it is the same here. Very often things do not sink in the first time, or possibly many times, and teachers have to be very patient about that. It is the normal situation.

With much love,
Ruth

September 17, 1989

My dearest person,

The more I think of our relationship and the in-depth and mutual love that we share for each other, the more I am convinced that there must have been an overwhelming bond forged between us long ago. In my last letter to you, I spoke of the love element as a desperate need that I depend on you for. After giving it much more thought, I realize that that statement holds more truth than I thought at first. When I met you, I was a very desperate person, and in many ways I still am. Shortly before meeting you I had been pushed to the point of deciding whether I should become a decent person, a submissive (broken) one, or a human animal. There is nothing in the prison environment that inspires decency as a human quality. In here submissive means total surrender of one's individuality. In short, this place breeds human animals, and in an effort to justify their brutality and atrocious behavior against prisoners, the prison employees will only depict prisoners as being animals to the outside world.

Yes, my love, in many ways, since meeting you, my desperation is more intense, but it is more positive and controlled. I am desperate not to become a human animal, I am desperate not to become submissive, I am desperate for truth and self-honesty, but the thing that I am desperate for most of all is the continuing close bond that exists between us. A great man once said that,

> Men who have never received and have had little occasion to express the love theme of original goodness respond in a very significant manner to that first real, spontaneous, gratuitous kindness. Those feelings that find no expression in desperate times store themselves up in great abundance, ripen, strengthen, and strain the walls of their repository to the utmost. Where the kindred spirit touches this wall it crumbles. No one responds to kindness, no one is more sensitive to it than the desperate man.

I think you will never know the great difference you have made in my life. You have made a difference in the way I treat others. You have made a difference in my thinking and in the way I view life in general. Sometimes even when I'm around others I feel like I'm alone. It's really sad to see and hear the false values and emphasis people place on material things and other things that don't matter. It is no wonder we fear each other as we do. Sometimes I feel like I've become a stranger among my brothers. How can one say to the stranger that we don't have to hate and kill each other because we don't look alike, think alike, and act alike? How can one say to the oppressors that until justice and peace is administered to all, the whole world lives in danger and on the brink of destruction? And how can one say to the enemy that it is my wish to love you, and if you will only give me a chance, I will show you how much easier it is to love rather than hate. Sometimes I still smile to keep from crying, for you have awakened something within me that I cannot explain; yet I know it is there, just as I know that I love you because I can feel it, and it is beautiful.

Your postcard is greatly appreciated and cherished, for it is a symbol of your love.

Lovingly,
Martin

———————

September 18, 1989

My very dear Ruth,

Thank God for people like Ellen, Tom, Diane, and your other friends. These are the kinds of friends and people that give meaning to our hope and faith in others and in the idea that we as a people will learn to live in peace and harmony as one instead of divided by our fears and hatreds.

I went to court yesterday and a very peculiar thing happened to me in the way of enlightenment. As I was standing before the judge, I tried to focus all of my attention, understanding, and energies into what the judge, prosecutor, and my public defender were saying. I was not only hearing their words, but also the underlying meaning of them. My public defender ceased his efforts to conceal he was working hand-in-hand with the prosecutor against me, and for a fraction of a second I felt a soul connection between the judge, the public defender and the prosecutor and myself, and it was gone just as quickly as it had appeared. These people know that the average guy, who comes into that courtroom charged with battering correctional officers, is no more guilty than they are, but they will exhaust the taxpayers' money trying to prove an innocent man guilty. I think by maintaining my silence and not trusting my public defender enough to confide in him, I am trying to tell them that I will not dignify their courtroom hypocrisy.

A prisoner was beaten nearly to death last week and the last I heard was that he is in a coma and not expected to live, and the doctors say that if he does live, he will only be like a human vegetable because of the extensive brain damage. The responsible parties (guards) are reportedly saying their action was justified because of the prisoner's aggressive behavior. In other words, he refused to be submissive; he refused to accept their physical brutality without trying to defend himself.

After standing before the judge yesterday with a courtroom

full of viewers, I was led back into the waiting room by armed guards. Even though the guards are armed, I am still led into the courtroom in leg shackles, handcuffs, a waist chain and a handcuff metal box to restrict body movement. Taking someone into the courtroom with all of these mechanical restraints is like telling the jurors this person is so dangerous and irrational in behavior that it is necessary to restrain him as such. This is not true in all cases. One has to wonder if a jury can be unbiased in view of such an obvious and broad statement.

I am enclosing the response I received from the library. It seems they misunderstood my letter because their answer has nothing to do with my question.

You mean so much to me and you are a great beacon in my life. Your love is very sustaining, and I love you more than I can say.

To Ruth/Mom with my heart,
Martin

———

September 18, 1989

Dearest Martin,

It certainly looks as though there is a plot against your using the library. How little control one has there over one's life. It is a little scary. My suggestion is to pay for the books they claim you lost. I can probably send the money tomorrow. When you offer it, you should make clear that you are not guilty of losing the books, but that you want to clear the air and be able to continue borrowing books.

Experience has taught me that people who are manipulative and have power will stop at nothing to get their way. And they will put on a great show of pretending to be your friend while knifing you in the back. It is not just the books that I think about, but the fact that you are in a "war zone," subject to any of their whims, no matter how brutal.

Our greatest support in difficult times is Christ. He and the angels are looking after you. It is not just the present situation and your desires that are important, but the accomplishment of something more that can happen if we listen. A great many people have made great sacrifices for reforms, and there is still so very far to go. Mostly there must come a change of heart. I feel how easy it is for me to be writing about it from the safety of my room, and I have to admit I am sometimes frightened for you, in spite of my faith and determination to be accepting of what comes. We can't even write privately. I will be doing a lot of praying and a great part of it will be, "Thy will be done."

I'm very touched by your writing "adopted mother" on the package permit request form after "relationship." What a dear you are and how I love you!

I have been thinking of how the teaching is more important than the teacher. It is truth which must, in the end, stand up by itself.

Perhaps you think it strange that I told you to pay for the books. Here one has to think not of one's emotional reaction to what people do, but of what, from a deeper sense, is the best thing. In this instance, one turns the other cheek—one returns good for evil, not out of weakness, but out of strength. It is not what others think that is important, but what you think, what is true, and what makes sense. If people don't recognize it, and you do the right thing, then you are right with yourself and with God. Who else do you need to please? Not even me. The fact is you will please me whatever you do because all this is for you to think about (or meditate about) and then decide for yourself. It is your life, your deed. If there is a lesson to be learned, it will be your lesson. One should, then, make it clear in a statement with the offer of payment, that you did not lose the books but want to clear the air and continue to borrow books. If they are lying, they will know it. You do not need to try to convince them, in any case. You can say the truth, then let it go.

There were many instances in my life when people chose to believe things of me that were not true. At one time I would have tried to explain. Then I realized that explanations in such instances were useless. I let it go. Some will find out only after death, when they do a review of the past life, and when they see things as they really are. I found that I did not have to make everything right, but rather leave some things in God's capable hands. If we do the best that we can in life and if we try for the good and the true, that is what counts. We do not need to please the ignorant, and we do not need to live according to anyone else's ignorant rules. Independence and strength are things inside of you. You also do not need to disclose your inner being to anyone, regardless of what they think. Remember the quote from Hermes, "Seal it in your heart . . . "

At times the Jewish mother part of me feels concerned, but now I am at ease, truly leaving it in God's hands—and sometimes also in yours. I send you heaps of love and a thousand hugs to last a while. Don't use them all up at once. I will send some money for the books and if it is not enough, do ask. Do I need to remind you that mothers can be asked?

Love, dear son,
Ruth/Mom

September 20, 1989

My darling son,

Lately I have been waking from sleep very slowly, with a feeling of having been far, far away. And I am in no hurry, but want to linger in the quiet and peace that surrounds and fills me. And in the middle of the night, last night, when I awoke, it was as if I was in that far away place and could look at things, people, questions, and see a bit more than usual. I saw our love, which was so very deep and beautiful, and it had in it the element of freedom. It was the love of mother and son, and it did not bind in any way. It wanted nothing except to have love flowing freely without demands or desire.

And as I looked at you, it seemed that you were under attack. I surrounded you with a large ball of protective light and felt that you were safe, but then the light was gone. As it was going, I saw you as a very young child, and I held you in my arms to protect you with my own back from blows aimed at you. And then you were grown, kneeling down with your arms up around your head, in protective gesture. Then I saw you stand upright, straight and tall, your arms at your sides, unafraid. It was dark, but only so that one could somewhat see. And you just stood. It was not so much a physical form. The darkness penetrated everything, even the space where you stood, as if I was not looking at a physical body, yet you were definitely there. And I noticed around the periphery, low down, a little distance from you, many dark figures—

just the upper torsos and heads—but like dark shadow figures. I realized it was a kind of prophecy. I would stay back and leave you free—be with you, but not interfere. It would not be my body, nor my light that protects you, but your own. You are not the child, but the grown man, who will gradually awaken light within himself. And that light will shine beyond your own body to fill the space all around where you stand. It is dark still. The work has only just begun. I saw how in the future the light within and around you would shine bright and the prison walls would fall away from around you, and you would be free.

I have thought about what you wrote in your last letter about love. You are a loving being. You need to love, for it is what you are. That love, and the light, are one. You will awaken it, for it is very strong and it is already there. All that holds it back is fear. When you know that you do not need to please any but yourself and God, the rest will come.

I will close so this can go out in today's mail. Someday, when we meet, we will have much to say that cannot be put into letters.

I love you so very much,
Ruth

CHAPTER 9

Togetherness

September 21, 1989

Dearest,

My last letter said I would not intervene in the future, but for now I am still here, still writing, still holding your hand, and sending more hugs in case you used up the last batch. I look at you and try to see how you are faring and I can see that you are sitting quietly on your bunk, in deep contemplation, letting all the new ideas work in you, sorting things out in your mind and heart, letting the eyes of your spirit come to life inside, helping you to find a direction. There is no hurry and I stand by. You are right about the close bond between us. Yet I let you be yourself, do your own growing, make your own decisions, leave you free, lovingly. Our togetherness comes from a very far past, way beyond when I was your mother, and it will be there into the infinite future. We have a mutual task, and the close bond that exists between us is living reality. Questioning is fine. The more you question, the more you will find out for yourself. I do not expect anything different from you than what you are. Be truly yourself. Find your self.

Yes, your new awakening does, in a way, make one feel estranged from one's brothers, but only outwardly, until "you find your way to one another through the spirit." First there is the separateness, aloneness, differentness, the abyss, where there is no "ground under one's feet"—all stages to be gone through, not permanent. The deceit, the cruelty, the harming of one another, all those things you experience in prison are, in certain ways, out here, too, though there is also goodness and love and helping.

And for now, love, hugs, blessings, everything good and beautiful.

Ruth/Mom

———

September 22, 1989

My darling Ruth,

Only with you can I discuss and share my most intimate thoughts, my fears and hungers, my weaknesses and strengths. You are the first person I have met whom I do not fear, and this is a love so beautiful and pure in essence that even I cannot fully comprehend it sometimes. I am most thankful that you are a part of my life.

Your advice concerning drawing back and looking at things from a less personal point of view is indeed a very good and helpful method of dealing with the daily annoyances and irritations.

You are absolutely correct about there never being any privacy in here. Also, in the years that I have been here, I have been constantly strip-searched, and it is still a degrading and dehumanizing feeling, just as it was the first time it happened.

Loneliness has also been a very difficult lesson for me. You are my closest companion ever, and from the beginning of our letters and your book, I experienced a joy and freedom so great until it felt like these were my first moments of happiness and love. I remember feeling that you were someone I have always known.

I hug you and say many thank-yous and tell you how much I love you, my very dearest.

To Ruth/Mom, with love,
Martin

———

September 23, 1989

Darling,

I appreciate, very much, the confidence you express toward me by sharing your experiences there. Two things impressed me very much—the moment of soul connection you felt with the judge, public defender and prosecutor, for one. I hope it will be further developed. The other is your silence as a way of expressing that you will not dignify their courtroom hypocrisy.

It is known that incidents of prisoners being beaten to death do happen. It is a sad commentary of our times that people do not rise up against such things. Yet it must change, unfortunately slowly.

You are right about the library's answer not making any sense. When there is such a block as is happening in regard to your getting books or an education, then I suppose it is best to wait for now, for a better time. It makes me wonder if I am right in my feeling not to send you material from the copier at this time. I don't want to call attention to the one way I've had of sending things to you.

The picture of you with all those shackles, plus armed guards, does not leave me. I have had all sorts of thoughts and feelings about it, from weeping to laughing—laughing because it seems so ridiculous. But this morning I do not laugh because an idea has occurred to me. I wonder if the drama of so many shackles plus armed guards, plus pushing you around in that situation when you could easily be unbalanced and fall, is not only to impress the jury, but to make you angry. One more outburst from you could well be your last. If there are now laws against keeping prisoners drugged without their consent, there seem to be none against murder. I am also thinking about the concerted effort to prevent you from getting books or an education. In their idiot minds anyone who wants an education must be a threat. I pray for you, but it is you who is the one that needs the courage, presence of mind, love, and inner strength to withstand the onslaught. In the midst of it all, I see you finding inner quiet and peace. I continue to surround you with protective light.

About the remarks of the prisoner we write to: He does not believe in absolutes. He holds the common view that truth is what you think it is and therefore it is different for each person.

There is this quote from Dr. Steiner, "Truth, like math, cannot be voted upon in parliamentary fashion."

Know you are much loved and carried in my heart,
Ruth/Mom

September 26, 1989

Dearest,

I went ocean watching today in Pacific Grove. This area has a rocky coast, unlike the sandy beach of Carmel. Some people are feeding the little ones—ground squirrels, sea gulls, cormorants, pigeons and many different kinds of birds, large and small, that I can't name. I am sitting on a bench very close to the water, listening to it speak and writing this letter. The squirrels live in holes between the rocks and they keep skittering about, getting peanuts and carrying them off into their holes. I counted about fifteen at one time, but since they are not quiet for long, it is hard to tell. They come to me, too, and I apologize for not having anything. I put out my hand and some put their paws on it to see, and they sit up on their hind legs and sniff. One took my finger for a moment.

It is later and the people are gone and some squirrels are still coming to me hopefully, sitting up, staring at me, walking on my foot. Some are sitting about, sunning on the rocks. They do not stay long in one place but move about. Off in the distance are several sailboats. One motorboat is moving swiftly. Sometimes there are sea otters here, but it is hard to see them among the seaweed. How beautiful it is here! I take you with me in mind and heart. The foghorn is nearby. When it is foggy, it's loud enough to blast one out to sea. A natural promontory goes a distance out into the sea and one can sometimes walk far out. But then it is necessary to watch not to get stranded when the tide comes back in.

How I love you,
Ruth

2:00 AM—September 28, 1989

Dearest Martin,

I awoke dreaming of you, and of how much anger you carry in you, and I see how, if they kill you in prison, it could still be your own anger that kills you. It is not so much what is happening from outside, but what you carry within, that needs to be conquered.

Pictures are trying to stir in me, and they are of us in a life together as young companions, sister and brother, being torn apart. Such love we have had, for so long! I only see it dimly, as if looking at it from very far away, and it is hard to make it out. Whatever the past was, that brought about such intense anger, it is you who suffer the effects, and it does nothing to further your growth but only holds you back. When you overcome it, the growth will be enormous. You also carry a great amount of love, and the two are doing battle. The love will have to win out, of course. It is the greater force, and it is supported by our Christ.

I see everything that is happening (or has happened) as making so very much sense—the skin color, the difficult childhood, your violent anger. I can see how you, yourself, have chosen it in order to develop certain characteristics that you will one day be able to use productively. And an important part of it is the time you are spending just where you are, in a "cell." Cell is the right word here, not referring so much to a prison cell as to a place of a kind of new birth—an embryo developing. How right the meditation is for you that starts out, "Inner work has outer effect . . . "

How much I love you and how privileged I feel to be your companion. Again and again I see us reaching out to each other and being pulled apart. This is all. And I imagine us being together again. How much of this do you sense? How can you strengthen your own loving nature in order to bring about a healing? Now I am speaking of love in general, rather than what goes out to a particular individual. Perhaps we are not together at this time just in order to develop a wider love that will include all the world. When we experience our love, and enlarge it toward others, isn't that what we are doing?

Later—I went to sleep after writing the above, and now the memory is here. Sometimes one begins to experience a memory as if it were very far away, and bit by bit it comes closer and becomes more visible. It can happen over a long period of time. At first one only senses it and becomes aware of a feeling connected with it. Several weeks ago, when I awoke in the night (these experiences came every night), my nerves were in an almost unbearable state. I was sometimes soaking wet with perspiration. There was crying in me, and sobbing, but only silently. I have never been able to scream and have tried to do it in the woods where there was no one to hear, but no sound comes, also when I cry. I kept feeling myself reaching out to you, and for a few moments we are together, usually in a big, open field, and then the picture is gone.

Now I see us as children together, sister and brother, very close, very loving, always together. Later we fell in love. How difficult, how painful it is to remember and to write. It is our family, then, who separated us. I need not tell you of the pain of that separation and the inconsolable longing I feel. As the memory came, I wanted to say that one can die of a broken heart, for I did, but I realize it was helped along with doses of arsenic. I had become pregnant and such a situation could not be tolerated in a "respectable" family. I was locked away in a remote part of a large house, alone, sometimes not fed, with nothing to do and nothing else to think about but my loss.

I see you among many other boys, evidently having been sent away to school. I am not sure of the place, perhaps England? I think it was not too bad for you at school because, although you suffered deeply, you were occupied and active with schooling and companions. The real pain, then, came when you returned after some time and learned what had happened at home. By that time I was long dead.

In these weeks, without knowing why, I have been reaching out to you with such longing. It should heal now. One must not carry so much past. I am crying inside this morning, but no one will know, and it will not last. Time to put it all away and go on with the new life that is coming here. We must put the past to rest. Then we, too, can rest. What I wrote to you about experiencing joy and beauty and humor is doubly important to help bring healing. That you still carry so much love in you is wonderful. Love is the greatest healer of all. Christ teaches us that, especially at the crucifixion. Christ gives love without being loved back, and we must learn that, too.

We have been together, deeply loving, oh, so many times!

Ruth

———————

Evening—September 28, 1989

My darling,

After writing the earlier letter to you this morning, I received such a dear letter from you saying that from the beginning you felt I was someone you have always known. I spend a lot of time alone now, resting, and the days are filled with you and with the knowledge of our having known and loved each other forever.

I feel the pain deeply and I find no rest and cannot sleep. I wonder how many such nights you have had in prison all these years, and especially in confinement. How much hopelessness, how many days and nights of nothing to look forward to? How have you borne it, what kept you alive? The memory that has finally surfaced is deep and oh, so painful. It has made me feel even closer to you if that is possible. It eases as I sit up with the light on, writing to you. I try to experience, not what was lost, but the love we feel, and I copy from your letter, what I, too, feel—"I am most thankful and blessed that you are a part of my life, my heart, my love, my thoughts and so much more." That is what I shall try to concentrate on when I again turn off the light and try to sleep. I will tell myself that as soon as I fall asleep, we can be together. How did you know six days ago when you wrote those words, that just tonight I would need them?

September 29—Yes, it helped to think, not of the loss, but of the love, not the pain, but of the miracle of finding each other. And what a miracle it is! And it is a miracle, also, that you seemed to know at once that there was something special between us. When the pain wants to come, I will fill myself with our love instead, and gratitude that we are in the same world at the same time and that we are allowed our letters— as many as we like. I no longer share your letters. Does that seem odd? We seem to have entered a place that belongs just to the two of us.

September 30—Another night and the story goes on. I awoke in a great sweat, remembering it. This time it is about your return. It seems a long time later—you had been kept away for as long as possible—several years, it seems. At first no one would tell you what happened, but you gradually drew the story, bit by bit, from a couple of maiden aunts. In that day it was usual for aristocratic families to stay together in big old mansions. As you learned the truth, your anger became enormous. It seems that it was then that the young lad, who had been one of the most gentle and loving beings, began to change into someone who could become violently and uncontrollably angry. You left the family then, and it is not clear where you went or what you did. You may have been a wanderer. And as you had contact with other people, the disgust you felt at people's callousness and cruelty, which began with your family, grew ever stronger, for you found people everywhere to be the same.

How interesting that your present life has been one of contact with just those people, just those characteristics, you abhor. It is as if you have been given what you need in order to overcome in yourself what holds you back. The only thing that can set you free is to deal with it within yourself, to overcome your own disgust, anger, hatred, and especially fear. It is fear of people that you have lately spoken of, that I am the only one you do not fear. Even when our feelings are justified, we must not be carried away. It is the Christ we must follow. And how close he is, for I found him in your cell. What was I looking for then? Wasn't it for the ability to "love them all"?

Yesterday was a quiet day. I was alone most of the day. There was so much sadness and quiet, oddly, almost peaceful sadness, so very deep and far beyond the personal. The experience that happened so long ago is so close tonight, and I wonder if you will feel any of it, or if you will be able to relate to it? I feel so much love for you it makes tears well up. I cry for us—our love, our pain, our separation and loss. I cry with the longing to see you again. I cry for a child who was never born. Be sad too, my love, sadness is all right, but exchange your anger for love. Be a totally loving being again, the young boy who was my son so very, very long ago.

See things, see people, as they are. Do not give up true seeing, but see with understanding and compassion. I, too, am trying to learn these things along with you. I go to you, sit in your cell with you, and see Christ there with you. He blesses us and we are his children, belonging to him.

It is like I have been far away these days of remembering, and a bit like recovering from an illness. How very dear you are to me!

I love you so,
Ruth

———————

September 29, 1989

My darling Ruth,

In response to your letter of September 20, your visions bespeak of many things that I feel but did not know how to put into words. I, too, sometimes feel very strongly that I am somehow being prepared to perform some special kind of task later on in this life. The hardest lesson for me to learn at the moment is how to respond to evil without responding in kind.

There have been many things in this life that have caused me much pain and suffering, and I'm sure there will be many more, but since you have come into my life, certain veils have been removed. As a result, my mind has opened up more. I am pondering and attempting to act out things so as to make them a natural part of me for the betterment of all. In the sense that only you might understand, I am very consciously aware this morning that pain and suffering are enforcers of growth. Who would ever have thought that we would one day bow our heads in humbleness and give thanks for our pains and sufferings! So you see, my beautiful, you are responsible for such thoughts that proceed from the recesses of my mind. Ah, if you could only look into my heart, if you could envision the loneliness that lived there before you, the lies, deceit and treachery that were a part of my make-up, and if you could know the beautiful feelings that come over me at the purity and sincerity of your love, then you would know that words cannot express my love and affection.

The money arrived for the books. My better senses tell me that the way you are suggesting is a brilliant way, even though I cannot see it yet. I will fill out a request slip tonight. Before I do I will pray or meditate so that I might proceed without malice, but instead with clarity of thought.

Please realize that you are not helpless and inadequate in my case. You have caused a very violent and hostile person, me, to revise his thinking and actions, to re-evaluate himself rather than blame others for all of his failings and short-comings. By listening to you with my soul as well as ears, the change in me is apparent even to me. Your statement of turn-ing the other cheek out of strength, not weakness, is monu-mental wisdom. It has given me insight into my daily activities and other things.

And now my loving and lovable Jewish mother, I will say I love you dearly. Your hugs are most comforting and warm. Your letters mean so much to me.

Love,
Martin

October 1, 1989

My darling Martin,

I have read your good letter over and over. The mood of the past memory stays with me and, as I know from previous such experiences, it will gradually fade. It is the love we share that stands out most of all and that will stay and grow.

I think of your mother putting you out because you tell her you will not let her beat you, and what a sadness that is. How blind she is not to have seen the love she could have had from her son. What a loss to her. I go to you so many times and you are such a comfort to me.

The nights are still difficult, when memories return with more insight and with certain fears in this life explained by that other time. Everything was handled so roughly, without any sensitivity, cruelly. The only feeling I seem to have toward them is to be as far away from them as possible, no hatred or anger, nothing at all except a wish not to ever be near them, whoever they are.

I love you so very much,
Ruth

October 1, 1989

My darling,

The reason I went to court the last time was that the court wanted to know why I refused to see the court-appointed psychologist that they sent here to the prison to see me. Since I refused to talk with him, they were attempting to diagnose my mental state themselves by asking me a lot of silly questions, such as, have you ever been to trial before, Mr. Forrest? My reply was yes, I have been on trial every day of my life. The judge, "I am sure, Mr. Forrest, that we are all on trial here." I am not really sure what he said after that because the thought that entered my mind was, "I wonder if the one who is judging you is as biased as you are? Do you feel that no matter what you say, the odds have already been stacked against you?" These were the questions that came to me, but I kept them to myself because I felt they would not understand. After I went silent on them, the judge postponed my trial date, which had been scheduled for the following week.

I feel that the prison officials here are doing their best against me to help the court get an easy conviction. Anytime a prisoner offends an employee of the prison system, he offends the whole system. If there has ever been such a thing as a close-knit family, then the prison system and its employees are a good example of this. An officer once told me in a philosophical manner that "We, as correctional officials, are not always right, but we are never wrong." That statement was made some years ago, but the memory of it still lingers fresh in my mind. And I suspect it will always be there because it was made by one who represents almost absolute power and authority over the helpless.

Yes, my love, it is possible for one to experience joy, beauty, and love in a place like this if one learns to see beyond the surface of everyday life. Like anything else it has to be practiced and practiced until it becomes a natural part of you. It makes life worth living. You are the only reason I am able to see beyond the horror, treachery, and deceit that are so prevalent in this environment, and I am actually able to laugh sometimes at the extremely serious outlook that I and others take when going about our daily life. Just as you suggest, laughter most definitely has a curing quality, and I find it easier to laugh now.

To Mom with love,
Martin

October 5, 1989

My darling Ruth,

I am still astounded by the ability you have to make me take a closer look at myself rather than holding the world responsible for all of my shortcomings and failings. Before you I would defy and rebel against things that I knew were right just for the sake of maintaining my stubbornness. It was as though everything and everybody presented a challenge to me that I felt a need to overcome or I feared I would be conquered by them. And the fact of the matter is that this thought pattern must have started at an early age for it to be as deeply imbedded as it is. I'm sure it started with my mother, because I can still remember so vividly the many times as a kid she would shame me by beating me and chastising me before all of my young friends. Sometimes this fear of being totally subdued resurfaces and I tend to strike out or fight it with violence and hostility, for those are the only ways I knew until you came along. Now I am learning to deal with this fear with patience, understanding, gentleness, wisdom, love, and so on.

My memories and visions of the past are next to nil, but for a very long time, I have felt strongly that I have been closely associated with a female in the past. Even though she did not have a name and I could not picture her face, I felt she was probably on earth at this time. And, if I ever met her, I would know her because there would be certain things that I would be able to tell her, express to her—without shame, without fear—since we have traveled this road before. You and only you, fit this description perfectly, and it is only with you that I am free to be my complete self. When I wrote to you in one of my earlier letters that "From the beginning I felt that you were someone that I have always known," these thoughts and feelings were occupying my consciousness very strongly.

Both your letters written on September 29 are beautifully narrated, strong, revealing, and they express so much. Since my relationship with you, I have experienced the beauty of being so very, very close to another in thought, mind, soul, and love. You remind me of myself, when I'm writing to you. I, too, sit for long periods of time, just dreaming and feeling very close. There are times when I get to the point of feeling your presence. Then I feel that we are doing and thinking along the same lines at the same time.

Your memory of the past most certainly does have meaning for me. It makes a lot of things that have happened to me a lot more understandable. When I was in the county jail the last time, I had a deep craving for reading material concerning the royal families in the old country. It seemed like I had to saturate myself with this type of material constantly before I could satisfy this craving. I read love novels and a lot of nonfiction books based on historical data, and anything I could get my hands on concerning English royalty.

I received the reading material and the stamps and your three beautiful heartwarming letters. I thank you for your love, your trust, and all the other inspiring qualities.

To Ruth/Mom, with all my heart,
Martin

October 8, 1989

My dear Martin,

Something you said set my mind thinking. To quote: "It was as though everything and everybody presented a challenge to me that I felt a need to overcome, or I feared I would be conquered by them." I think it goes beyond your childhood experience with your mother into the whole question of freedom. It seems to me to touch on what the soul is struggling with in an inner effort to evolve and become an individual, truly awakened being.

Your statement is profound. The world wants to shape and form us into its idea of what we should be. Whether in prison, or not, there are restrictions and restraints that try to keep us from being or becoming true individuals. Another quote from you: "You and I are very much alike in the sense that we are in less control of our lives than we would like to be." I think of all the restraints on you, the many shackles that are put on you when you leave your already confining cell. These are thoughts and pictures that stay with me. They are pictures of what the soul experiences. It is like an outer representation of the inner struggle of man. Things are given to us, or shown to us, on various levels, and the physical world is the arena in which deeper things are able to be enacted in order to awaken us. Such could be the hidden meaning of the outer restraints. First there is the experience and only later the understanding.

Yes, of course, there is physical freedom, and that is what you refer to when you say we are less in control of our lives than we would like to be. But the other expression—the fear of being conquered by them—that seems to me to go deeper, and I hear in it the cry of the soul wanting to be inwardly free. And that we can be no matter what outer restrictions there are. For inner freedom we need to find the key, not to a place of magic where all our wishes are gratified, but to a place of hard work, difficult problems, and hurdles to overcome. It is where the transformation takes place from lower egoism to the higher self, the spirit individuality.

There is a being inside of us which can stand tall, which is not subject to the will and whim of outer circumstances, where anger and violence are not in control, nor the ups and downs of the emotional effects of what others do or say around us. It is a place of calm and peace and balance, a place where we are in touch with the reality of spirit and nature. There our feelings and thoughts are ours, our acts, our speech, our love and laughter, altogether our own. That inner self, the true self, that is what must not be allowed to be conquered. That is the real task of this age. It is not made easy, and that is how it must be, for it is only through being exercised that it can be brought into being and made strong.

For the present, we may have to hide this inner work of

ours from a world which wants everyone to be like itself, which is not tolerant of anything different, even of beauty and good sense. Become beautiful inside. Think true thoughts. Be loving and caring, not with strain and intensity, but lightly and gently like a bird in the air. Not at once will it happen, not even in one lifetime, but we can make it our aim. And each time we seem to fail, we can pull ourselves patiently, lovingly back to try again. Do it alone inside, in solitude, where Christ may be your only companion.

Know that I love you very, very much
Ruth

———————

October 11, 1989

My darling Martin,

Very soon after we started writing you spoke of how comfortable you felt writing to me. I was surprised that you felt that way so soon. It is no longer surprising, because the soul knows no barriers of space or time. When we meet someone in person, it is no surprise to sometimes feel a sense of recognition at once. Why not by letter? It took me a little longer, and it seemed to happen gradually. And then it really blossomed with my first memory and grew even deeper with the second. I think your anger matched the intensity of our love. How understandable it is. And now you have the great task of keeping the love and letting go of the anger. In the end it will have been by the fact that you had anger and finally rid yourself of it that contributes to your growth and the possibility of becoming a free being. Then, one can think that perhaps other people, in their violence, cruelty, and destructiveness are also on such a path. What an odd idea. And how strange, then, is evolution. That is an interesting thought—that some people take on the worst characteristics in order to finally transform them. Such a task must be done for the whole. There is the beautiful statement that the rose adorns the garden when it adorns itself.

I decided it was time to do some color work on your mail.

It has been too long. So you get the brightest sunburst that I can manage on page one of this letter.

Mountains of love,
Ruth

<hr />

October 12, 1989

My darling Ruth,

Last night I had a beautiful and rather strange dream about you. It went like this: There was another guy trying desperately to gun me down, and just when he was about to do it, you appeared like magic, out of nowhere and said to him, "Young man put that gun away. My son has too much love in him for him to die such a brutal death." The strange part is that the guy actually put the gun away, even though he was trying to kill me as if his life depended on it. You were very soft-spoken in your request, but yet you spoke with authority that none can resist. After he put the gun away, the three of us took turns hugging each other. It was a very beautiful dream, one which I shall always cherish. I have since been meditating upon it in an effort to derive a better understanding of it.

The signals from the librarian are now very clear that there are to be no books. They answer my offers to pay for the ones they claim I lost with gibberish. One can file grievances, and even carry it into the courts, but it will accomplish nothing if they are determined to have their way.

Love to Ruth/Mom, with my heart,
Martin

<hr />

October 13, 1989

My dear Martin,

This night when I awoke there were no words for you—only love. After a while I turned on the light and there, beside my head, between the lamp and the bed, was a fine web and the spider who made it. He is a daddy-long-legs. In the morning he must go outside, and I have told him so. I have already put out others, who evidently want to come in from the coming winter. I have told him about Dr. Schweitzer, who wrote about reverence for all life.

Are you familiar with the writings of Maya Angelou? I saw her on TV a couple of times and fell in love. The little library in my home town never had such books, but I have access to better literature here and last night the lady who works on the outreach program brought two books by her. I could not wait and opened one right away. And what a surprise to open to a description of her meeting with the artist Varda, a wonderful Greek character I knew long ago in Monterey when I first came to this area. Her writing is as great as she herself appears to be on television.

I am looking at some of your letters and in one you wrote, "The hardest lesson is that one need not respond at all." All that is necessary is to recognize it within yourself, see what is there, and let it go. Build up your own being within you so that you are not swayed by what comes at you from outside, but remain as separate self, strong and clear inside. Then one looks out and "sees," but inwardly remains intact. In that way you strengthen your own loving nature and bring about a healing.

Something very special happens when two people truly love each other. It grows until it includes all of the world.

So much love,
Ruth/Mom

CHAPTER 10

Restraints and Obstacles

October 18, 1989

My dearest love,

Sometimes it takes a very long time for your mail to get to me. Maybe the officials are up to their old tricks again. They have a reputation for tampering with and withholding guys' mail.

I went to court on the fifteenth. The judge had a court-appointed psychologist waiting to interview me. At the beginning of the interview, the psychologist asked me why I refused to cooperate with my public defender so far? My response was, "Why should I cooperate with someone who is working with others to deprive me of my freedom?" This was really the extent of the conversation, or interview, because after this first question, the psychologist told me that it was not my place to ask questions but rather to only answer them. I ceased talking to him altogether because I realized there was nothing I could say that would be beneficial to my situation.

After the interview he told the judge that because I had refused to talk to him at length, he could not give an honest, professional opinion. He went on to say that since I refused to answer any more of his questions, it was his personal opinion that I was feigning mental illness; therefore, he was highly recommending that I be placed in a mental institution for a period of observation. Naturally the judge went along with him. I fail to see how placing me in a mental institution is going to influence me to cooperate with someone I know is working against me. I'm not sure when I'll be leaving, but it will probably be real soon. I am sure that there is a deeper meaning and purpose behind this sudden turn of events, and I am presently trying to absorb and understand as much as I possibly can. Life without understanding is no life at all.

I think you have an innate talent for putting into words

things that others cannot. The most amazing thing about it is that you have explained something to me that I did not quite understand myself. It concerns the statement I made: "It was as though everything and everybody presented a challenge to me, etc." I have even expressed that thought to some of the guys up here, that physical conquest is very insignificant when we consider the spiritual aspect of freedom. Yes, my dearest one, there are all types of restraints and obstacles placed in our life path, and I am rather sure that physical bondage or prison is the least of them. It can be justly said that prison is where I began my journey toward absolute freedom, thanks to you.

The being that you speak of, the one that can stand tall and is not subject to the will and whim of outer circumstances, this is the one that I have been trying to preserve in my own way, by violent and rebellious means. Even though I did not understand it as you have just explained it to me, I realize that this is what I have been fighting for, but in the wrong way. You're a doll and I love you and thank you.

I received an answer from the U.S. Department of Education, Office of Student Financial Assistance in Washington, D.C., along with the necessary application forms to apply for financial assistance for schooling. Evidently the institution officials here are monitoring my mail because they intercepted this material and sent a note along with it telling me I would not be allowed to take any education courses. It would seem that officials would be promoting education for prisoners, but this is not the case. Tonight I will make a special effort to send love to all opposition.

To Ruth/Mom, with love,
Martin

———————

October 18, 1989

Dearest,

I'll write again soon, but right now I want to say we've had no damage from the earthquake, although its center was very close and the house shook badly. We have no electricity and we expect it will be off for a few days. That means no heat, since electricity controls the thermostat on our gas heater. Our electric cooking stove is off as well.

Last night we had dinner by candlelight around the coffee table in front of the fireplace—several kinds of cheese and crackers, sweet potatoes cooked in the fireplace, sweet corn cooked in their husks in the hot embers, and steak for Tom. We felt very lucky.

Afterward we went by the ocean and watched a beautiful sunset, with the ocean the calmest I have ever seen it here. It seems odd that we escaped damage when there is so much in Santa Cruz and San Francisco. They tell me it is because we are on solid rock here.

I love you much, always,
Ruth

October 23, 1989

Dearest Martin,

I laughingly agree that you really went overboard with the colors on that envelope. It looks to me like a struggle between anger, joy, love, and a lot of thinking. Joy and love have to win in the end because they are more fun. And isn't it better to be happy? Color does speak!

Please use the money I sent you to pay for the library books for anything you like. I'm sorry they will not let you spend it on food. I had hoped you might be able to get a special treat.

Sorry about the books. I think we can honestly assume it is intentional. There's nothing much they can do to you in your present circumstances except the little annoying things that have been happening—your cell searches, delaying your letters. Suddenly I realized the answer, and it is so simple and obvious that I smile at me for not being aware of it before. You have committed the unforgivable crime. You beat up a guard. It doesn't matter what he did to you or was about to do again—what is it an officer said to you, "We may not always be right, but we are never wrong?" You still have one defense only and that is your inner work. Can you see their side? Put out all sense of right or wrong, or even what makes sense. Look at their side, from their point of view. They are a group, a clan, an army. Prisoners are the opposition, to be controlled. They are the power, they are in control, and they are always right. It is not in their consciousness to be humane. You need do nothing with this information except to see it as it is and to accept its reality. It is fact. Prisons are, for the most part, not correctional institutions. It is where officials are permitted to commit every possible crime and still feel innocent because they are the power. I'm sure it never occurs to them that they are behaving criminally.

All this time pages five and six of *Love Can Open Prison Doors* are on my mind. He is being mercilessly beaten and, " . . . in an unbidden instant there welled up within me an overwhelming compassion for these men, for their pathetic ignorance, their undeveloped souls, for the pitiful condition of their minds and hearts."

I'm doing much praying for you and sending good wishes; keep having good, loving feelings and thoughts. I shall read the Starr Daily book again to help me remember how to love the opposition and the ones who cannot understand. It is right here, ready at hand.

It is quite a while since I sent you anything for your collection of sayings, so here's one from Ralph Waldo Emerson:

> There is only one success—to be able to spend your life in your own way. To laugh often and much; to win respect of intelligent people and affection of children; to earn the appreciation of honest critics and endure the betrayal of false friends; to appreciate beauty; to find the best in others; to leave the world a bit better, whether by a healthy child, a garden patch, or a redeemed social condition; to know even one life has breathed easier because you have lived. This is to have succeeded.

Love,
Ruth

———

October 28, 1989

My darling Ruth,

The winter season seems to have reached this part of the earth overnight. Along with its fiery coldness it has brought about a lot of changes. We have been given our winter clothing, two blankets, extra socks, a jacket, and two teeshirts. The buildings are equipped with a central heating system that is very adequate whenever they decide to use it.

I smile at your sudden awareness of the reason for a lot of the annoying things that have been happening. As you say, it is so simple and obvious. I beat up a guard. Sometimes it is even lost on me, and this is very unusual because it has always been my code to be aware of the consequences whenever I encounter this type of trouble with anyone, especially the correctional officials. Once a person commits such an act against a correctional guard he automatically becomes a traditional enemy. When I first arrived at this institution, one of the guards told me that I had better keep my eyes open at all times because the incident was far from being over. I had the overwhelming impression that they were going to outright kill me, and I still think that they were trying to do exactly that.

These people are very shrewd in their killing methods. Most of the time, rather than doing it themselves, they get other prisoners to do their killings for them. To give you an example of how they set guys up to get killed I am going to recite to you the facts concerning eighty percent of the murders that go on here. According to the prison officials, every person that is presently housed on this wing poses some kind of threat to their system. Of course, they have other confinement wings, but they are not considered as big a threat as the guys on my wing. Therefore, any time a person is brought out of his cell here he is brought out handcuffed behind his back, and he has on leg shackles, waist chains, and a black box. While these guys are being escorted down the long hallway by a correctional guard, they have to pass through a horde of other prisoners who are not in restraints and who have access to various weapons. If any of these guys who are not in restraints should decide to strike with the intent to commit murder, the guy in restraints is totally at his mercy. Out of the last ten people that have been killed here, eight of them have been killed in restraints while being escorted down the hallway by guards, and in every instance, the guards have either run or stood there and watched the prisoner die.

After finding out why I was transferred, a prisoner warned me not to be in a hurry to be escorted down the hallway because it could be a set-up. And true to this person's warning, these people seemed intent on getting me to go on some kind of medical call out for the first month I was here. We do have a choice of deciding to go or not. When they stopped trying to get me to go on these call outs, this feeling of their trying to set me up to be killed gradually faded. This was during the time I first started practicing sending love to all of them during my meditation sessions at night.

Love is most definitely a very powerful force, and I am greatly blessed and most thankful to have been introduced to it by you. Until you, I could only equate love with romance, sentimentalism, and lovemaking. These were the only aspects of love that I had been introduced to, and my consideration for others and my thinking was very limited. I never knew how much I was missing. I reread the pages of *Love Can Open Prison Doors* that you suggested, and I am again impressed by the power that this revelation carries, even more so now than when I read it before, because I have experienced this over-whelming compassion, love and forgiveness. I think that truth will always be felt even if it is not understood.

To Ruth/Mom, with love,
Martin

———————————

November 2, 1989

My dearest,

Yesterday the guards came and told me I had a medical call out, and I told them I did not want to go because I did not feel sick, nor did I request any medical attention. They then told me to turn around to be handcuffed because they were moving me to another confinement wing. When I began to pack my personal belongings, they told me not to worry about it because they would do it for me. I knew then that something wasn't right, and I thought they might want to confiscate my legal documents that I have been trying to keep safe, or that they have come to silence me forever as they have many others. The only fear that I suffered from was "What will I ever do without my Ruth," and yes, this is one of the foremost thoughts that can reduce me to tears without shame. In this environment it really is a shame for a grown man to cry. As you can see, I am very much alive. They have me in a cell without any of my personal belongings. The wing where I am now is where they keep the prisoners who supposedly suffer from some kind of mental disorder. I am laughing now as I think about being here. I had to borrow this paper and pen from the fellow next door to write this letter. I have been trying to get them to at least give me writing materials since yesterday, but they have refused all my requests, so I give up and go to my next door neighbor, who turns out to be an old acquaintance. Lucky me!

Know that there is always the possibility that I will suddenly leave this world as I have lived it, violently. Sometimes this is an overwhelming feeling that I can't seem to shake. If this should happen, it is my prayer, hope, and wish that I will leave in the spiritual and mental state that you have so lovingly blessed me with, and as I am now, without malice or the cry of revenge and without fear. If this is to be my fate, know that I wish to depart from the world as I was born into it, with the cosmic understanding that all life is one and that all people regardless of their race, creed, or station in life, have a destiny to fulfill in life. And I would pray that whatever happens, I would be fulfilling mine as was promised by the wise spirits who giveth all things for a time and take them away, only to give more and better things.

Now I say good night and rest in peace. Perhaps we will meet in the dream world. I can never say it enough—

Love yah so much!
Martin

November 3, 1989

My dearest Martin,

This morning I am thinking about our relationship and the first word that comes to me is *trust*. I don't think that needs any description, do you? Then I think of *love*. And what more shall we say that we have not already said about love? And then there is *support*. It means we will always be there for one another, always available. What else is there that is not covered by trust, love, and support? One can write volumes about them, or nothing. Between us there is so much understanding that maybe nothing is necessary. I had the question recently: "If we were together, would there ever be anything about which we might have any problem?" And I smile. Why would there ever be anger, or any such thing, if there is no block, no fear, no opposition, no misunderstanding, no door closed to listening and hearing. Then if there is to be a better world, it must be just those characteristics that need to be cultivated/nurtured.

It is a lovely day. Tom made some phone calls to pick out a good camera for me at a price I felt I could pay. He knows cameras and knew what to ask for. Then I went downtown and bought it. This afternoon a friend drove me to beautiful Point Lobos, where I went crazy with the new camera, snapping everything in sight. If they are good, they will be headed for you. The camera is fully automatic and quite compact. You put in the film and close the cover, and it buzzes itself to the first picture. Then all you do is point it in the direction you want and push the button. It then automatically winds itself to the next picture. At the end, it rewinds itself, and you take out the film and put in another. Isn't the modern world wonderful?

Your letter of the 28th came today, and I am a bit shocked at your description of the murders that take place there. I knew they kill there, but it is still shocking to hear it firsthand from someone so close to me and personally in danger. It made me frightened for you, of course, but horrified in general. Still, keep me informed. I want to know the reality and I hope you will feel you can always tell me everything. I am training myself not to worry about you, but to constantly see you in God's hands and know that all is right with you no matter what. Keep up your good work. I'm so very pleased with your progress.

And I love you so very, very much,
Ruth/Mom

November 4, 1989

My darling Ruth,

I am still in an empty cell without any of my personal belongings. I guess they are still telling me that they have only
themselves to answer to when it comes down to running their
system. It's fine with me, but I must still be myself, my individual self, with the best of my ability. Anything less is unac-
ceptable. I am more than positive that without your guidance
I would be fighting them at this very moment, like a fool.
Because of you I don't even have the desire to do so anymore.
I often laugh at my tough guy image and how it will quickly
bow down to your beautiful presence.

I feel guilty about giving your address to someone when
they moved me the other day, even though I know you don't
mind. But if anything should happen to me in the manner I
described and you should hear from me no more, then you
would know why. You are probably the one person that I
would have taken the care to keep informed. My other family
members have been conditioned to the point of accepting
almost anything they are told by any certified authority figure,
especially chaplains, reverends, and so on. I know it would be
useless to try to explain the situation to them in its reality.
Believe me, I have already tried. They only like hearing nice
things from me, even to the point of telling me that if I can't
write about nice things, I shouldn't bother writing at all. So
they almost never hear from me, not out of spite, but rather
from lack of communication.

I love so very much the study you, Iris, and Diane are doing
together. How I wish that I could join you. I will always be
there with you in spirit, anyway.

My love and hellos to the family,
Martin

———

November 8, 1989

Dearest,

They have returned all of my personal belongings, along with
the legal documents. The only reason I can think of for their

taking them is to stay abreast of the evidence that I will present to the courts when (if) I ever have an opportunity. The doctor who is in charge of this wing is the person who is most responsible for having my belongings returned to me. He interviews everyone assigned to this confinement wing. After observing him the few days I have been here, I almost couldn't believe the continuing patience and endurance that he exercises in dealing with people.

Your letter of October 27 arrived a couple of days ago, along with many beautiful goodies. The foremost are the darling pictures of your little dog, Lily, and the beautiful story to go with them. I have read the story and looked at the pictures over and over, and each time it produces a beautiful and warm glow such as the one Lily experienced when being reacquainted with her friend the butterfly. The story is exceptionally beautiful. It creates magical and wonderful feelings in the soul.

The other items enclosed with your letter are some educational literature from Dr. Steiner, which I always look forward to with eagerness, some love stamps, and so on. Ahh, so many beautiful things! All of them are so very much appreciated. They keep me aware of things that I would otherwise have no knowledge of. I thank you dearly.

I thank you, also, for the beautiful selection of poetry you sent. I have been reading them over and over. I have a deep-seated love for poetry, and these are extremely beautiful. You are blessed to have known such beautiful and talented people, and I am highly blessed to know them through you. The Gods are truly good to me. I thank you for sending me the things you feel special about. After reading about Lily's death, I too, have cried for her. By your beautiful and warm memories and your so loving stories about her, Lily still lives for all of us to enjoy and fuss over. I thank you for sharing these stories of Lily with me.

Much love, my darling Ruth,
Martin

November 9, 1989

My dearest Martin,

I have a letter from you and one from your friend, to whom you gave my address when they moved you so suddenly. Apparently you are all right. I had thought of writing to the superintendent to ask in a friendly manner for a report on what is happening. My main reason would be to let him know that you have someone on the outside who is caring and looking after you. After the double-talk from them in answer to my previous correspondence about books, it is not likely they are the people from whom to get honest information about even more serious matters. But it seemed to me less likely that they would cause you harm if someone on the outside might cause a stir. And you can be sure, if anything happens to you, they will find they have a tiger by the tail or the equivalent. But I did not feel the need.

Pink walls. How nice! I think?

I remind you of the quote from Hermes: "Knowledge will be your strength, Faith your sword, Silence your impenetrable armor."

The pictures are the result of my first "happy snapping with the new camera." Tom said, "At first try everything. Don't be picky and try to be artistic, just take a lot of pictures. Find out what you and the camera can do." We did all right. The credit goes to the good camera and fine film and wonderful views of nature. How can one not do good in such beautiful surroundings? The squirrel came to pose and offered a front view of its face even though I asked for a side view. "That's my best side," it insisted, and you know it's no use trying to argue with a squirrel.

I am thinking, what if I were to write a poem just for you? What would I say? So I stop and do it. I am pleased because it expresses what you are and will accomplish. Sometimes one is able to bring something to expression successfully. Maybe the angels help. Maybe it is egotistical to be pleased with my own writing. We can say, "I suppose so," and then laugh at me. So here it is:

To One in Prison
Life has controlled you.
Now you learn to control it.
It has brought challenge.
Now you will meet that challenge
And make it your servant.
Your courage will become
A tool to fight for the good.
It is not physical fighting.
Courage is standing tall in the spirit.
The love you already carry,
Deep, strong, giving—
Your courage will let it come forth
Without fear, without holding it back.
People will see you and know:
It is all right to love and to care.
They will see in you that love
Is giving freely without conditions.
Teach by your acts, by the force itself
Of your love without desire.
Christ will be in your love.
I tell you about what you already have.
Like bringing it forth out of the wood or stone
As the sculptor does, so will you deepen,
Shape, and bring forth
Your courage and goodness and love.

Heaps of love to you, dear son,
Ruth

November 13, 1989

My dearest Ruth,

I am sending you my commitment papers whereby the judge
ordered me to be placed in the state hospital. I was informed
by a correctional official that the institution is in violation of
the court order in keeping me here. I don't know what all of
this means, nor am I worried about it. I suppose they will get
it right eventually.

It is after lunch. We had liver, rice, black-eyed peas mixed
with vegetables, biscuits, pineapple, and carrot salad. I don't
know if it was a delicious meal or not. I normally just consume

my food without the thought of how it tastes. I think if it tasted anything like it looked, it would be inedible. To give you an idea of the lack of concern in which the food is prepared, the guys are so used to finding roaches, bugs, and other things in the food until they have learned to become detached before eating it. I found two bugs in my food yesterday.

You asked about the black box. It is a small metal device used to clamp around the handcuffs to keep them more secure. It is about the size of a small Bible. Without it some guys can use a paper clip to take the cuffs off in the blink of an eye.

I will be sending you a package permit for whatever books you have in waiting. Most of the items on the permit we are not allowed to have, so to be on the safe side I am only going to ask for the books. I believe they will allow four.

Your envelopes with the colored drawings are really beautiful. They make me feel very loved and warm inside. I thank you dearly for showing me the way. I love you more than words can say.

Much love,
Martin

———————

November 13, 1989

Dearest Martin,

There is no end to learning, and I am still working on meditation. I am trying to work with faith and still finding it difficult after so many years. I had awakened with a certain fear—my body grows stiffer, there is more pain (not yet serious) but finding myself slowing down, less in control, worried me. And so I began to be aware of how faith is absolute trust, and I'm afraid mine is still a little distance away from absolute. My mind thinks it knows, but . . . So faith is my project for now.

You asked about the earthquake danger. Certain things are right for certain people. Things can happen anywhere at any time and this is my right place to be. I do not live with worry. We all have to go sometime. One can die in so many ways— in a car accident, in a plane, from a volcano or tornado, in a bed. A tree can fall on us. God will decide how and when I go. He will do it with Godly wisdom. I am much less concerned about death than being incapacitated. I must learn that God is in that, too.

This is the first time you have spoken about food. Yech! There is certainly a lot that needs correcting in the "correctional" institution. So that is why they use that term!

I suppose one can develop a sense of pity for those who take advantage of the less fortunate. They are certainly setting up a lot of karma for themselves. That one reacts strongly to such things is good. It surely must come from being a caring person. Anger seems to be quite justifiable in certain situations. It is what we do with it that makes the difference. Emotions are important and should not be restrained within. We need to be able to feel everything, but we must not let feelings control us. Let them flow inside. They are indicators and give us information and they are gifts from our creator. Train them and learn to use them in the right way.

Much, much love, my dear Martin,
Ruth

———————

November 16, 1989

My very special love,

Your letter of November 7 makes me vastly aware of the part we must all play in activating the love doctrine in this human experience. It also makes me anxious to speed up the process of my growth, for it is my ultimate wish to contribute as much as possible before leaving this body. I still hold to the philosophy that "to whom much is given, much is required." And yes, my compassionate one, by you I have been given much. In all humbleness and appreciation I say that I can now hear some of the things beyond the physical ear, and see some of the things beyond the naked eye.

You have described my feelings perfectly on the day they moved me when you said, "As we grow, we begin to carry in our being a feeling of acceptance about the things we can do nothing about." It is the kind of feeling I have been experiencing quite regularly lately. Before, I used to explode out of frustration, confusion, and my inability to correct things to my way of thinking. Your meaningful words are given in true understanding.

Yes, life is much different on this wing; there is a lot more activity. Most of these guys are on psychotropic medications. That makes them less of a physical challenge and they are treated more roughly by the guards. Some of them are really mentally unable to help themselves, and on the slightest provocation, they are taken downstairs and put into a strip cell with absolutely nothing on, or they are placed on a cement bed spread out in four-point restraints. There is a person across the hall from me who really has a problem mentally. The guards went into his cell the other night and roughed him up a bit, and then, they took him downstairs and put him on the cement bed. I asked one of the guards as objectively as possible why they put him on the cement bed, and he said, "Because the guy has a mental problem." He said it as though he really believed the cement bed was the answer to his problem. It's really scary the way some people think.

Love forever,
Martin

November 18, 1989

My dearest love,

Your curiosity concerning my height makes me laugh lovingly. I think it's really cute that you should ask. With much pleasure I tell you that I am five feet and eight inches in height and I weigh about one hundred sixty pounds. As for my looks, well I have never been called handsome, but I have been called ugly from time to time by some of the real choosy females. From the time that I first read that beauty lies only in the eyes of the beholder, I have stopped looking in the mirror so often. I wonder if it was an ugly sage that invented this wise saying so as to give us other ugly ones a way out.

I now have a big window in the back of my cell that I can look out of. I can watch the sunrise and the sunset. There is a big warehouse in the back and the place where they do all of the cooking for the institution, so I get to watch the guys move back and forth all day during the five working days.

Even though the thick screen at the window makes things kind of obscure, the window still gives me a variety of things to look at.

I am going to try to explain why the guards' behavior patterns and attitudes are determined by what confinement wing they are working. All of the confinement wings are placed in categories, classifications and characterizations, such as the death row wing, the violent wing, the nonviolent wing, and so on. Each wing is handled according to the nature of its classification. Before being assigned to a wing, the guards must go through a short briefing where they are advised of the calibre of the prisoners they will be dealing with. They are then instructed on how they should conduct themselves. So mostly, when they come to a wing, their attitudes are already fixed, kind of like a stiff collar. Since this wing is classified as housing the most aggressively violent prisoners, the guards naturally come prepared to deal with a violent atmosphere. Since another wing is classified as a psychiatric wing, they come prepared to deal with that, however improper their attitude might be in particular instances.

It is a beautiful thing you are doing in using different themes in your meditation, and especially in working with faith. The idea sounds so good and inspiring that I am going to start doing it. My favorite and most common themes are love, forgiveness, and oneness. Faith is a very powerful thing. I think, up to a certain point, all of us have it, as much as it takes for us to survive anyway, but not enough to liberate us from our petty desires and other ignorances. As I reflect back on my childhood, I can't think of anyone with more faith than a child. They are truly trusting beings. The other theme that sticks out foremost in my mind is freedom—spiritual freedom.

I love you,
Martin

November 22, 1989

My very dear Martin,

Your envelope of November 17 is especially dear. It is so gentle and full of love and joy and is an expression of you as I see you.

You told me you would not be given drugs against your will, so I assume you are not getting any. I would find that disturbing, as you know. There is so much that is barbaric in these supposedly "enlightened" times. I am also thinking of the cement bed and the kind of consciousness of the workers there. I wonder what karma is at work in these things? Of course, we make new karma, too. I have just been reading about the inquisition. Such horrors! And they still go on. Yes, I'm sure you are being given a very special training and there will be a task for you at the end of it. I must wait for a next life for my real task, for this life has been mostly preparation. I will be supportive of you, whether from this world or the next. My memories of you still give me much pleasure, of the time we were so close as mother and son, and then as sister and brother, and also of the meadow we played in. There are such beautiful places on earth, wonderful places. You will see them one day. Yes, my darling, grow quickly, because that is how you will be freed of that place and come to me.

The commitment papers make me laugh. I laugh about who is inside and who outside of the mental institution.

A letter from you recently said, "Who other than you would understand me when I say that I have experienced more freedom here in prison than anywhere else?" Thinking about you this morning I thought, "Who else but you would experience such freedom in a prison cell, in confinement?"

I love you dearly,
Ruth

———

November 28, 1989

My dearest Ruth,

Today's mail brought many blessings. There are three big envelopes from you. How wonderful! The designs on your envelopes are awesome, and I love every one of them. Thank you.

I am sure security has banned me from the recreation yard, for I have not been taken out with the others. I am sure the memory of what happened to one of their fellow workers by my hands is still fresh in their minds. If I were in their shoes, I might react the same way.

Sometimes I am almost startled at the accuracy and the good timing of your information and advice. I am referring to the things you say concerning our emotions. They are indeed indicators that speak to us and give us information. They are very good for letting us know some of the things we need to work on. In an earlier letter, I was telling you about one of the floor trustees who spit in the jailhouse lawyer's food. Well, for an instant I found myself feeling a slight satisfaction, thinking that perhaps the person was getting a taste of his own medicine. After thinking it through more thoroughly, I was ashamed because my thinking was just like the guy who spit in the food, which certainly wasn't good or helpful. Instead it only made him more bitter. Bitterness is one of the worst kinds of deaths that a person can live through.

I hug you many times,
Martin

———————

November 29, 1989

My darling Ruth,

Your discussion of fear makes me aware of things I did not think of before. In your words, "Should we not fear ignorance and prejudice? Should we fear cruelty?" It makes me wonder if fear should be completely overcome. Does not fear in some sense even exist for the Gods? I wonder?

Some further parts of the book you are sending have arrived, and some material about *Peace Pilgrim*, and love stamps and poems. I thank you dearly for sharing them with me.

The "higher ones" are constantly showing their concern and making themselves known by testing our growth. It seems that I am being tested by the same things that used to affect me so much in a negative way. Such a challenging journey this can be! But I love it, nevertheless. I am finding it more profitable to fight the bad things in me rather than fighting against uncontrollable outer forces. When I think of my darker days, I can remember the times that I would actually become overly disturbed at ideas that opposed my ideas of reality. I thank God that I have graduated from that stage.

Excuse me if this sounds macho, but I would never have thought that I would see the day when I would be telling a woman that she is the bravest person I know. It is only through you that I am beginning to perceive the spiritual essence of God.

To a loving mother,
Martin

CHAPTER 11

Do the Gods Weep?

December 5, 1989

Dearest Martin,

I don't know, my darling son, if fear exists in some way, for the Gods. I feel sure that Gods weep. Like everything in existence, there is a reason for all the emotions. God knew what he was doing when he created the world. This is certainly true of fear and anger. The question is, how do we use them? Is it in a constructive and useful way or do we go about punching people?

I should be concerned when you say your present wing is a more dangerous place to be than before, but I am not. I feel confident that you are being looked after, and that your own inner growth and love will protect you. I expect you will also take care. One must not expect the spirit world to do it all. It is unlikely that you will get out of confinement and back into life without going through danger. That whole prison seems like the thickest of a thick jungle.

I am smiling at what you say about sounding macho, in fact laughing. A man once said to me, when we were having a discussion, "You think like a man." Do you think he thought he was complimenting me? Prejudices can really be quite funny. One person told me I did not seem like a Jew, and in Germany, that I did not seem like an American.

I'm trying to think of new pictures to put on the envelopes. It's hard when one is not an artist and can't draw. No harm in trying. So if I have the courage, you may get some new ones, just designs. When I did the last one, of just mountains, I was thinking of a vision I had many years ago. I was in Europe at the time and in my late thirties. I had had many inner representative pictures of various times in life and this time I saw myself going over a mountain range. It was all mountains everywhere I could see, just one ridge after another. And every day I watched my progress, and it was always the same. Then I began to realize that I was approaching the highest part, and that when I reached the top, I would at last be able to see beyond. Daily I came closer until at last I stood on the topmost peak, and I looked with great expectation. What I saw was more of the same, nothing else as far and wide as I could see, just more mountains and valleys. I laughed then, and stopped watching. Similar to what they did physically in *The Long Walk*, I've been (in a soul way) over the Himalayas, through desert, through the deepest forests, through thick masses of brambles that were full of thorns and thistles that grabbed and scratched and tried to hold me back. Such pictures are not made up but are actual representative pictures that show what is happening in the soul.

I have been putting holes in some of the things I send you, so they can be put in a notebook if you wish. You will get covers when it feels safe. I hate to get things back, especially when letters are enclosed and have to be mailed over again and get to you so late. Some parts of the book I am sending you have been returned when I get pushy and send more than just a very few pages at a time, so I break it down to smaller parts and try again. Each time they send their form saying no books are allowed. I know that you get copies of the form without knowing what it is they have returned.

I send you much love and prayers, my dear son,
Ruth

———————

December 11, 1989

My dearest child,

I awoke in the night and you were re-experiencing, in a way reviewing, the experiences of the past—the hurt, anger, violence, beatings. This is something that happens in the process of healing. It is called retracing. It was not happening in any order, as far as I could see, but haphazardly, one thing and then another, sometimes several mixed. And I think that was because it was mostly on a feeling level and feeling could bring up a number of memories with which it might be connected.

I stood by, just being there with you, sometimes embracing you for a moment; sometimes we both embraced. It was happening on a spirit level and our touching did not stop on the boundary of the physical body. It was your experience, but I could share and support, lovingly, as a mother and friend and companion and be there very much with you in spirit.

When I looked at the clock, it was past 4:30 A.M. When we are working at overcoming something in ourselves, whether physical or emotional, in the process of healing, such old memories are released. It is a kind of discarding of the past, a freeing so we are ready to go on into a new future. It doesn't mean it will be easy, only that we drag along less old garbage. I like to think that for you it means there will be less anger, less hurt, less desire to strike back at the world.

It must have been about an hour later when I fell asleep again. I awoke feeling so much love and I called you child, not because you are a child, but because you are *my* child and very dear to me. For some reason, it is the beatings you received as child that I keep seeing—someone hitting you with a whip.

How very much you are accomplishing in a short time! It is true that I helped you, taught you, but you had to do the work yourself. I also tried with someone else who seemed receptive. (Otherwise I never would have done it.) Finally he rejected it and threw it in my face. He had shown signs of this along the way, but never clear. And he told me things, at last, that showed that he had been deceitful and manipulative, not really lying, but giving false impressions. Then, typically, he accused me of manipulation and of just those things that he had been doing. The point is that he is not ready to see himself, understandably, because it can be painful, and perhaps for him, with a long history of alcoholism, especially so. People are given opportunities and they can accept or reject them. The worst thing for him is his dishonesty. As the end of this century approaches, more and more people will have to make important choices. Those who respond will be given special help by the spirit world. A new impulse is coming for the world and those who hear it will become workers in a special way.

This person is still close to me, but our exchange has been reduced to mundane things and the weather. Things he tells me about his family are not nice, but he evidently takes them as normal, not knowing that there is such a thing as real caring, or not wearing masks, or growth on a deeper level. Something deep inside searches, but when it approaches him, he immediately cuts it off, and it was this seeming search that misled me. After his more honest revelations, he began to send loving cards, saying things like, "Life is brighter when I think of you." He was evidently afraid of losing me, and I must confess that I considered it. But not for long. I answer all his letters, send him love, which I still feel, and have conversations about what we do, but nothing on a deeper level. Now he says that he had taken an interest in my letters because he thought I needed someone to talk to and that he is a good listener. He couldn't be more wrong on both counts. I do not need someone to talk to and a good listener is one who truly hears. So I bless him and put our exchange on a casual level, which is all that it is.

I send you love, my dear,
Mom

December 12, 1989

My dearest Ruth,

I have just watched the last bit of the sun go down over the horizon. It is always a beautiful sight to behold.

Your questions concerning fear and anger are very thought provoking. I quote: "How do we use them? Is it in a constructive and useful way, or do we go about punching people? Do feelings control us or do we control them?" I, too, have been pondering them. Though I have improved very much, I realize that I have just begun.

I love so very much the way I feel free in expressing myself with you. Almost everyone else seems to want to compete in one way or another. Some of the guys in here are so insecure until you never know what is offensive to them. As for human relationships, things are dangerously off course. I am remembering the time I told you that qualities such as love, forgiveness, and other similar virtues could not be practiced in here because people would not understand them. Your beautiful and subtle teachings have made me realize how wrong I was.

Something that we both have in common is laughter. It

seems that I, too, am learning humor and joy round about my thirtieth year, and they are beautiful.

My darling, you are never dull and if you ever do repeat yourself, repeating gives it more meaning and makes it all the more clear, so do not let it be a problem.

Much love,
Martin

———————

December 14, 1989

Dearest,

More doctors—a psychologist and a psychiatrist—came to see me today. I suppose they were sent by the court. After talking with the psychologist, I asked him what did he think was the matter with me. He said that he didn't have the slightest idea, but he was sure that something is wrong because of the fact that I'm on the psychiatric wing. Because I have grown weary of playing these doctor and patient games, I refused to see the other two. I am not sure what they are looking for, but it seems to me that they need my cooperation before they can come to a conclusion.

I have received the four beautiful books that came with the package permit from you and Diane, and I'm ecstatically grateful.

My love, there is no doubt about the sincerity of our love. From the very beginning I knew that it was real. Even though this kind of thing was alien to my outer nature and senses, I could not deny the truth of what I felt deep within. The first time I picked up your book, a great joy and peace and over-whelming love and happiness seemed to come over me. It was as though your spirit jumped out of the book and engulfed me and I began to smile and feel happy like never before. I wanted to run and tell somebody about this strange thing that was happening to me, but what could I tell them? How could I explain this beautiful thing going on within me? Alas, I could not without them thinking I was insane. So I had to keep it all to myself. I really don't know how to explain it, but I have always known that someone like you would come into my life. I did not know when, where, or how, but somehow I just knew. So when we met, my soul began to dance in ecstasy to the ancient and silent spiritual hymn because an unwritten prophecy was being fulfilled. Are not these the things that are only confirmed by the soul! I have loved you always and forever.

To Mom with love,
Martin

———————

December 17, 1989

My darling Martin,

I am thinking about your last two letters, which came yesterday, and I have more thoughts. I am thinking about the way you are locked up in a room all the time, and how food is passed to you through an opening in the door; it made me think of the way Tibetan monks did that to themselves—had themselves locked up like that for years, out in the mountains, all alone, with a little food passed to them once a day. They spent their time meditating. I certainly would not recommend that for these times, but apparently you are having something somewhat similar. Since it is given to you, we surely can assume that it has a purpose, even if we do not know what it is.

I'm glad you realize the need for practicing love, forgiveness, and so on, in prison. It does not matter if anyone knows it or not. The important thing is that it is done. The spirit world knows it and can make use of it, and the kind of energy that is generated there eventually can grow and create more. The same thing happens with bad energy. It tends to feed on itself and create more. It is indeed very important what kind of atmosphere we create. On a larger scale it even has an effect on the weather. One of the lessons we learn on the path is that our activity stands by itself. It needs no recognition or approval. And we don't need to see any results. We just need to do our best and let it go, to put it in God's capable hands.

I laugh about the logic of the psychologist who assumes that there is something wrong with you because you are on the psychiatric wing. It is like assuming that if you encountered someone in the water, he must be a fish.

I love you lots, very lots,
Ruth/Mom

December 20, 1989

My dearest Ruth,

I have been wondering why they keep me here so long in view of the judge's orders to send me somewhere else. As for why they keep me inside of my cell all the time, it surely isn't an innocent reason. You see, the incident at the other institution was like a monumental insult to the whole Department of Corrections, because they mostly maintain control of the prisoners with brutality and fear. For a prisoner to rise up and strike back physically without fear is unthinkable. I should be thankful that so far I have gotten off lightly. By striking the guard the way I did, I gave them all the reason they needed to kill me and justify it in the courts.

I have resigned myself to the fact that my physical fate is in the hands of thoughtless people. I am learning to deal with being confined to this cell for however long they wish to keep me in here. Sometimes I get restless, but it is not a big deal. Some of the guys at this institution have been confined to their cells for more than twenty years. I guess you can say it's an accepted way of life.

I have now read *The Little Prince*, and I am very touched by the spiritual forces it stirs up within. It is profound and lasting and I feel so very blessed to have it for my very own. I send my deepest thanks.

I, too, am thoroughly spoiled by our active exchange of letters. Bless you, dear mother.

Much love and a very Happy New Year.
Martin

December 22, 1989

My very dearest son,

All your letters are very special to me, but the one that came today even special-*er*. Your description of how you felt when you got my book touched me so deeply it brought tears. Yes, we have known each other for a very, very long time, maybe always and forever, as you say. And it surely was a real recognition that you felt. When I remembered being your mother, and still whenever I think of you, it is as if we are like one being, completely tuned-in to each other. It seems we altogether understand each other and always shall. I think I told you that, as far back as I can remember, I always looked into people's faces, looking for someone. Once I dreamed that I stood on the busiest corner of downtown Chicago, where I was living at the time, intently looking into every face of the hundreds of people that were going by. It stopped eventually. But the longing in my heart never stopped. I guess it was like the feeling you had about someone coming into your life. I still have a longing to see you, be with you, yet I appreciate, and am grateful for, the miracle of having found you, and of having this dear contact by letter.

Something you once said touched me very deeply and made me feel especially close to you. It was that you were rereading my little booklet and that it made you realize why you loved me so much. You have a very unique way of expressing yourself. Your remark told me a great deal that no one else could/would have said or understood. This morning I am rather sad that people do not strive for real knowledge, and in fact avoid it. Of course, I know this, but it never fails to cause me pain, and what I have realized anew, and even more strongly, is the extent of this attitude.

Recently I discussed the world situation with a professional person and found him to be accepting of political immorality as if it is inevitable and acceptable and cannot be otherwise; he thinks the world is unchangeable. He is, in his own way, dear, kind, caring, yet he is not at all disturbed at our treatment of South America and other places around the world. He does not know that we helped to create Noriega, Castro, the recent oppressors in the Philippines, Hitler, the Shah in Iran, and so many others. He does not realize the nonsense of creating slums and then spending millions to tell people to say no to drugs, and then to build more and more prisons to lock away those who have grown up in those slums. He does not recognize that for our court system to practice injustice is a very scary situation, and so much more.

I did not say much at the time. What does one say to these well-educated professionals who are the leaders and teachers of the young—the future generations? They are not listening at the moment. Someday it will touch them, if not in this life, then in the future. Until then, and as long as they see the world as purely materialistic, without spiritual reality, there will be little change. We need to learn to think of human beings as individuals—each precious and unique—not as so many numbers or statistics, as is so prevalent these days, with the accompanying attitude that it is perfectly all right for some to "fall through the cracks." So, for a little while, I will let myself dwell on these things and remember how much work needs to be done in the world and in ourselves and allow myself to feel a bit sad.

Much, much love I send to you,
Ruth

<hr>

December 30, 1989

Dearest Martin,

Thanks, my dear, for a so lovely Christmas card and poem. More and more, it seems to me, that your true self, which is warm and loving, is able to come forth. I think you were right when you said that fear played a big role in your behavior, but when you say you fail miserably because of your impatience, I smile because your progress is remarkable and rare.

I'm so glad you like the books, and I hope you will keep trying to get more whenever you can. There are so many I want to share with you, and I really cannot stop wishing for things to change for you and the book ban to be lifted and, also, for you to have an opportunity to get some education. What I find unforgivable is for people to be stopped from getting an education on their own. How can they possibly rationalize such a thing?

Much love, my darling,
Ruth

<hr>

December 31, 1989

My beloved Ruth,

Tonight is the last night of 1989, and I seem to be more aware of this fact at the end of the year than at any other time. Truly the year has been very blessed and most fruitful, and I have much to be thankful for.

Sometimes I catch myself staring at nothing in particular, smiling, thinking of you. And I know that the angels have really been very good to me, for they have shown me true joy, true love and happiness, even in the deepest pits of hell.

I spent the day in celebration by going over our letters and all of the things that you have sent to me. The beautiful feelings are just as strong as when I first got them. Before this year comes to an end, I would like to thank you for introducing me to the divine forces of the universe. I would like to thank you for being my wise and gentle teacher, my dear, kind and loving mother, my friend and confidante, and most importantly, my companion.

There is something that I want to share with you tonight and I'm not sure I can explain it very well, nor do I know what it means, but I do know that the feelings are very real. Twice within the last two weeks I have had sudden feelings of something like flashbacks concerning this thing that is happening between us. It's not the visual kind, but rather more of a feeling of familiarity, of the deep love, understanding, and rapport that we have. It's like I have experienced all of this before, but the memory of it was gone. The first time it happened I almost called out your name without thinking. The second time was just a few minutes ago. Both times I was in the midst of writing you a letter. It was as though I knew you as I know myself, and just as suddenly as the feelings came, they went away.

Just recently I have learned, through experience, that one

can generate and inspire love, strength, courage, and other fine qualities in another person as you do with me. I have found a freedom more liberating, more joyful and sustaining within prison than I have ever known outside of it. That is not to say that I do not look forward to being released one day. It's like I know it's going to happen, so I don't worry about it.

With you in mind, I say thank you and goodbye to such a beautiful and fruitful year, 1989. You make me feel so alive. Happy New Year, my dearest.

Love yah,
Martin

January 1, 1990

Dearest Son,

In a few minutes it will be the end of the first day of the new year. I hope it will be an important and good year for you. All day I have been trying to think of what to say to you and nothing special comes. I've sent you many hugs and held your hand and wished for changes that will lead to freedom in God's way and time.

If the guards catch you smiling to yourself, it shouldn't surprise them. After all, you are in the mental wing. I still laugh when I think of the psychiatrist saying there must be something wrong with you or you wouldn't be there.

It means much to me that you love the books I love. I have another book for you called *Kinship With All Life*. It is about communicating with all forms of life, and it was the movie dog, Strongheart, who taught the author how to do this. It was a wonderful little dog, of no particular breed, who taught me the same thing, but still I found the book very enlightening. I know it will be especially meaningful to you because you were so tuned in to all of nature when you were my son.

I have spoken to you about exercises you can do to develop this kind of listening, and how they have to do with lovingly observing, with care, the forms, movement, gestures, and sounds of the things you want to know about. Now I wonder if I also made sure that you understand the importance of being in full control so you can stop it, too. You should only use it as an exercise for getting more understanding. As you open yourself up to greater "hearing/seeing," you must be able to shut it off, as well. We do not want to become so "open" that we are overpowered by the feelings and impressions around us that come at us from outside. It can leave us too exposed and cause serious discomfort.

Much love, my beloved son,
Ruth/Mom

––––––––––

January 2, 1990

My very dearest Ruth,

You have shed much light for me concerning the ancient and present day meditative exercises. The way you have explained it has given me more clarity. I started using the lotus position a while back because I saw some guy in a book about yoga exercises in this position while meditating, and I just naturally assumed that this was probably the best position to meditate in. I am now doing it just sitting. The crazy part about it is that I had to constantly practice that position until my joints got used to it, and all the time, I was wondering what are the advantages of meditating like this. Thanks to you I now know that there aren't any advantages, nor is the lotus position necessarily good for these times and for the west. My soul rejoices in the clarity of your statement, "Not dreaminess, but more awareness is what is needed today, not drawing away from the physical world, but greater consciousness, more understanding of how to live in the world with more caring and love, not turning off thinking, but making it into a spiritual activity." Your advice concerning the lotus position, and not doing anything directly that would deal with the chakras, is most dearly appreciated. The truth of what you say concerning these things is felt within the core of my being.

My endless love,
Martin

CHAPTER 12

Court of Injustice

January 9, 1990

My dearest Ruth,

I was called to outside court yesterday, and it was a strange and far-out experience. The court said that there was some kind of mix-up in the last psychological evaluation, so I guess that means we have to go through the whole process again. For the first half of the day, all I could think of was how good it felt to be out of this cell. After I got over the excitement of it, I spent the second half of the day trying to listen from within. I was listening to the things that were being said and the things that weren't, from the guards and prisoners alike. The guards were noticeably more at ease when expressing themselves because of their authority and the power it gives them over the inmates. The guards never overlook their opportunity to emphasize to the prisoner that they are in sole control with their power of authority, and, therefore, all of their actions, however cruel and unjust they may be, cannot be wrong.

There were nine prisoners going to court yesterday and every one of them was charged with assault and battery on a correctional guard. The public defender, who represents all nine of the guys, told them that they were fighting a losing battle against the Department of Corrections. He told them that they would come out better by pleading guilty to halve the time that they would get if they were to take their case before a jury and lose. He assured them that they would surely lose in front of a jury, and he was thoroughly convincing. The prisoners seemed to accept this with a hostile acceptance, and the guards were indifferent. When it was my turn to stand before the judge, I broke my code of silence. I told the judge that he is not the guardian of justice as his title implies, but rather the judge of a corrupt system and, as such, he is helping to build upon a controlled and unseen violence that lives in the heart of every person who has been treated unfairly by his courtroom. I told him, in front of the whole courtroom full of people, that if he convicts one innocent person, he convicts many others because when this violence comes to a head, it will affect many others. I told him that by his actions he is no better than the worst criminal that stands before him. After I got through speaking, the judge assured me that he was going to send some more doctors out to the prison to see me.

I did not know that I would say all of these things, nor did I plan them. When the judge asked me if I wished to make a statement, something within me seemed to click and the words just came pouring out. When I began to speak before the court, I knew that I was not speaking out of sympathy or personal concern for myself, but rather for the betterment of humanity.

After paying attention to the people inside of the courtroom yesterday, the feelings that came to me were anger and fear. There didn't seem to be any feelings of remorse and regret for the wrongs that the people were being accused of, and I wondered why. I know that my statement only served to anger them all the more, and I like to think that was not my intention. It just felt like something that needed saying.

Your beautiful letters are pouring in like rain. Just as the dry earth is nourished by the raindrops, your letters are a great nourishment to me. They are always so rich and full of life. The many cruelties that go on in this environment sometimes kill a portion of the good that we are building up within me, but this isn't for long because your letters bring these feelings back alive with more force and a stronger conviction.

Thanks for all the many goodies—the articles about education, homeopathy, the pamphlets about Native Americans from a trip, beautiful prints of some plants, the beautiful greeting card with the angel on it, and, of course, your letters and stamps and various clippings. All of these things are dearly appreciated. As I sit here writing, it is another one of those times when my feelings of love and appreciation are beyond words. I never would have thought that so much love, trust, and happiness could be communicated this way.

I shall soon have a description and a drawing of my cell for you. I find it interesting that you should ask, and I am deeply touched by your wanting to know. The doctors and the guards have been complimenting me all week long on the unique way that I have my cell decorated. I have recently added the angel garlands that Diane sent to me, bless her beautiful heart.

You always do and say things that move my heart to tears of love and gratefulness. Your saying that you have never thought of me as criminal is a great boost. I like to imagine that that part of my life is over. Every day I am working to make this more than an idea and a wish, but a way of life. I think there is no better place to practice being noncriminal than in a place full of criminals.

The psychiatrist and his assistants make a routine check at each of the cells every morning. They look inside of the cells, ask us how we are doing, and write our comments down on their pads. I usually avoid saying anything to them because they seem determined to interpret the things I say in a distorted fashion. For instance, the new psychiatrist came by the other morning and looked inside. The nurse commented on the neatness of my cell, and he said that either I was a neat guy or that I was suffering from some kind of schizophrenic disorder which makes me fanatically clean. And then, he asked me why was I keeping my cell so neat? Without missing a beat, I told him that I was always getting uninvited guests. Would you believe that he actually looked at me as if there might be some help for me after all!

When it gets cold, like it did for Christmas, there is no such thing as keeping warm. It's impossible for us to close our windows because of the steel screens inside of our cells, and the prison officials have so far refused to close them from the outside. This was my reason for slowing my writing pace down until after the holidays. It was too cold to write.

To my Mom, with much love,
Martin

———————

January 13, 1990

My wonderful darling,

Here is another example of how tuned in we are to each other. I had been feeling how you would one day begin to remember our past connections and sure enough, your next letter spoke of flashbacks in feeling. Yes, that is definitely one way that it happens. How well you express it when you say, "It was as if I knew you as I know myself." When we were together, we needed no words. Even now we are tuned in in a way I have with no one else that I can think of. It seems especially remarkable when you think about how different our backgrounds are in this life. Doesn't it seem amazing to you? In a way we have so little in common. Yet what we do have is the most important thing of all. Imagine, we have surely loved each other for thousands of years, in many different roles.

It took a couple of readings to try to grasp what your letter of January 9 was saying. I have the impression it was very courageous to speak as you did in court, and that you were helped by the angels to say something that needed to be said. A vital element in it was that it was not for yourself that you spoke. How well I understand your anger and fear. Yet it must not have been out of anger that you spoke, but out of the truth.

You have made a fine inroad into "hearing" more than people usually hear when you describe the impressions of the courtroom. The more you can experience without emotionalism, the more good you will be able to do. Know the difference between emotionalism and feeling. Let what you say come out of the real situation without anger or emotion, but out of truth itself. Then God and the angels also have an opportunity to speak through you. It is good to have your thoughts clear, your caring and love inside you from the meditations and exercises that you regularly do, and then to meet situations that come up in the best way that you can.

Do not be discouraged if they do not understand what you say. Truth has an effect whether those around you understand it or not. Do not be concerned with results. Just do the best you can and let it go. (I hope you will forgive my repeating this important material.) If you see results, fine, but the most important thing is the right deed and the pure heart.

Thanks so much for sharing this experience. I take it into my heart and prayers.

God bless and keep you, my beloved son,
Ruth/Mom

January 15, 1990

My dearest Mom,

I am marvelling at how subtle true knowledge can be. A lot of the things that you say in your letters, and the reading material that you send to me, affect me a lot more than I originally thought. I have noticed that lately, whenever I am talking to others and doing things in general, I find myself putting into motion the ideas and exercises that you give me without planning to do so beforehand. Once I realize what I am doing, I try to put more heart and soul into it. In this manner, I realize that I am building up a more positive attitude—a stronger hope and faith for my fellow man. My heart, mind, and soul smile as I tell you that, from you, I have learned that if one such as I can be helped, then there is hope for most.

The booklet of your poems is a darling and beautiful surprise. It warms my heart very greatly to know that you have taken the time to think of others and to share this beauty with them. It will always be among my most cherished possessions.

When I consider the great love and understanding we have between us, especially considering the differences in our background, ethnic make-up, our educational differences, and our different stations in life, I am more than amazed. I am sure that what we have defies the deep falsity upon which our social status system revolves. I feel certain that there is a profound message in our relationship.

I, too, am looking forward to my next package permit with a great zest. It will be in March. I have managed to get some of the guys on the wing excited over some of my study materials. A few even go so far as practicing some of the moral exercises. Some of them, in their brief moments of joy and happiness, will suddenly do something very thoughtful and kind for the person next to them, whom they have previously called the vilest of names. Whenever I witness these kinds of happenings, I can only think of you with much love and thankfulness. When we reach out to help the stranger, we are in turn helping ourselves, and in this way giving and receiving are truly the same.

To Mom, with my heart,
Martin

January 16, 1990

My dear Martin,

I am looking at your picture, wondering what you look like now. What warmth, gentleness and sweetness there is in your smile. I'm so glad to have this picture even though it is rather dark and was taken so long ago. When I imagine us together, there is no sense of age or color, or anything other than that we are two alike souls. And then there seems to be nothing to say, just a lot of loving feeling and the wonder of the miracle of our love.

I awoke this morning with the word justice on my mind and realized how this word has so little meaning in the courtrooms these days. Of course, there are still those who treasure justice, but so many, especially those connected with criminal matters and prisons, have become places of buying and selling and trading, and of politics and power. No wonder they put you with the mentally disturbed.

Every time you speak of "assaulting an officer" there, I think about calling things by their right names. Out in the world, what usually happens in these assault situations, would be called self-defense. There is that old saying, "Might makes right" and, apparently, nowhere is that more evident than in prisons.

I thought it might be interesting to look up the word *macho*. It says, "ostentatiously manly." So I looked up *ostentatious*, and that said, "a showy display intended to impress people."

I think it is pretty obvious why you are considered mentally ill. Anyone who does not conform to their accepted codes is abnormal. I have thought of a term for the courts—not court of justice, but court of injustice. But to think that way makes us seem weird. These people really believe their way of thinking is right, and most people easily accept the way things are. So one who goes against the stream must be crazy. If there was one person who could see color among all others who were color blind, he would be the oddball and treated as such, and so it might be wise to say nothing about his difference and let them think he is like them. I see no reason why you should not do what is reasonably necessary not to stimulate attack, while not compromising your beliefs. And perhaps you have thought about what you might *choose* to do if attacked, if your instincts don't take over. You might still make the same decision, but at least it will be *you*, yourself, doing it.

You said the things being offered to you never rebuked with harshness, but of course! If a teaching is to be real/true, then it must practice what it says. If one speaks of love, then one must do it lovingly. A newspaper photographer in San Francisco once got a picture of a demonstrator hitting a policeman over the head with her peace sign.

Love, always,
Ruth, Mom

———————

January 18, 1990

My darling Ruth,

The sun is shining kind of bright today, and I have been standing at my window for the last thirty minutes or so absorbing some of its beautiful rays. I have been thinking and experiencing the fact that knowledge and understanding and the application of them is a very liberating and illuminating process, and the more we acquire of them, the more we begin to divest ourselves of our lower and insignificant desires.

For reasons I am not sure of, I have been dwelling upon the overwhelming feelings of pain that you sensed when you first visited your prisoner friend at the prison. Fear, violence, hostility, and pain are apparently more prevalent in the prison environment than any of the more positive feelings and thoughts. I am sure this is what makes it so hard to relax in here, especially if you are not used to it. Even for me, the state of relaxation is almost an impossible thing to accomplish, and I have been practically raised in the prison environment. The only place I can ever let my guard down is inside of my cell, and even in here, I have to really work at it because I am always getting unexpected visitors—the guards, doctors, and so on. They are always looking for the worst, never anything positive, especially in my case, because I have been refusing to cooperate with them in this legal situation that they have pending against me. They want me to act like a defendant by going to court to defend myself against the very charges that they are guilty of. I will not do it! The only thing at this stage of awareness that I feel the need to defend myself against is ignorance and fear. They want me to plead guilty to something that I do not feel guilty about. It does not correlate with my present understanding and philosophy of what truth and courage are.

Sometimes when I sit back and ponder the situation as a whole, I can't help but laugh. The funny thing is that from the legal standpoint, they feel that they must find me sane or insane. They know I am not insane, but my refusing to consult with my public defender automatically throws their judicial program and thinking off balance. As it stands now, their legal process is in a state of confusion concerning me. I feel very sure that they are screening all of my letters, word for word, going and coming. It's the little things that they do that makes me feel that way. For instance, sometimes when they are passing out the mail, they give the other guys their mail and then make it a point to tell me that if I have any, it hasn't gotten here yet, and then two hours later they realize that I have some after all. Sometimes they wait and let it pile up to four or five letters and then decide to give them to me.

Last night they came into my cell under the pretense of looking for a weapon. As small as the cell is, it took them almost two hours to realize that there wasn't a weapon in here. They left my cell in shambles. I do believe that my decorating my cell the way I had it was not in accordance with their psychological assessment of me. So now I'll fix it back up to their satisfaction to keep them from taking all my property. You know, in many ways I am glad to be here and to be experiencing these things because they are affording me a close-up study of myself and others. I am absolutely sure that I am at the point where I must outgrow my basic and conventional fears and ignorances or be mastered by them. And that is an unthinkable thought.

Lately, anytime something happens that opposes my likes and desires, I have been summoning all of my strength to give thanks for making me realize that these are not needs and maybe I am becoming too attached to them, therefore, these lessons are reminders to keep me on the right path. I came to this conclusion shortly after the guards got through dismantling my cell. Suddenly my heart lit up with appreciation and understanding of the part they were playing in my growth process. It was really in my heart when I told them thank you.

I now realize why I have rejected all the teachings that were given to me by others. All of the time I have been looking and waiting for you because it was predestined that no one but you and your teachings should do. I am just as sure of this fact as I am of the day and the night. I am lovingly amused at your reminding me that you are also a person with faults and problems, and so on. That is what makes me love you so much. It is because you are human, because you have faults and problems and, most importantly, you have the courage to acknowledge these things and grow. From the very beginning, something deep within me knew that you were the one I could walk with without the thought of competing. I knew that you were the one I could talk to with my soul without fear of being laughed at and persecuted. I knew that you were the one I could cry to without a sense of shame. I knew that with you, all I have to be is what I am, no more and no less, and for this I will be loved.

If I appear to be going a bit overboard sometimes in expressing my great love and reverence for you, it is only because these expressions are in my heart and soul and these words are the least of what I feel. You see, my dearest, before you came into my life, I had never experienced love without desire, I had never before known true kindness. I could not imagine giving without expecting something in return. Your teaching me and enlightening me to these divine qualities is like opening up the doors of heaven to one who has only known hell. For me, these are more blessings than my poor soul can contain.

I almost forgot to let you know that I have received the letters with parts of *Kinship With All Life* enclosed, and I am going crazy with love, wonder, and amazement for the wonderful dog, Strongheart. You never cease to amaze me with the things you send. For the last couple of nights, I have been going to sleep loving, thinking, and breathing that beautiful being. Wow, what a companion! What a book!

A new doctor here seems to be a very disturbed person. Last week I watched him stand and witness a brutal beating of a prisoner at the hands of the guards. After they beat him beyond resistance, the doctor ordered them to put the prisoner on a cement bed in four-point restraints. I am sure that the other prisoners watched the entire incident, because it was mostly staged for our viewing—to keep the rest of us in our place, so to speak. While listening to the prisoner scream and yell from pain, I knew beyond a doubt that if I could, I would gladly have made efforts to help him.

Know that I love you very, very much,
Martin

———————

My dearest son,

How nice it is to get letters every day for so long, and all so beautiful! They show so much growth and understanding.

That you are able to laugh at the behavior of these grown up juveniles and that you can take disturbing events as lessons is all to the good. I imagine that coming into your cell to look for a weapon could only be a pretext for messing it up. Or maybe they are looking for something in your mail and in your cell. I cannot imagine what it might be? And as for your mail coming all at once or late, I suppose it doesn't much matter in your situation. If they are reading our mail, what must they think of it? That makes me laugh, especially. We should certainly not take any of this seriously.

In our souls we want to relate to people. And when they play these silly games, how can we? The soul does feel a sense of hurt and loss and aloneness. We want understanding and maturity. You must have wanted that from your parents, as all children surely do. I do not need to tell you of the sense of loss when it is not there and of how deeply and irreparably it is imprinted. I'm sure all prisoners suffer from that. I imagine the longing and frustration and anger remains, and the few who can overcome such damage are able to realize that they must create for themselves what was not given. It requires a strong sense of independence and a willingness to be alone and the courage to be different and stand one's ground when attacked. It is necessary to feel sure of oneself and not really care whether others understand or not. I still remember how I wanted understanding from each of my husbands (and others, too). I didn't need agreement, only hearing. But when others around you seem blind, deaf, and dumb, one feels really isolated, pushed away, annihilated.

Once when I was playing with one of my little dogs, I began

to pretend I did not see her when she was right before me. There was a terrible moment of panic and I immediately picked her up and comforted her. A doggie doesn't have the consciousness to deal with such a thing. Actually most people do not, as well. Maybe that is what is required of you in that cell surrounded by ignorance, stupidity, violence, pettiness. Maybe you must be the sober, sane, independent, mature, grown person in a crazy place. About this I am not joking. Maybe you can disconnect yourself from their games and see the childish behavior and expect nothing else. If you expect intelligence, sense, logic, honesty, goodness, justice, you will be sadly disappointed. If you see what is there and recognize where they are coming from and not look for what is not there and learn to love them anyway, then you can concentrate on your own growth. Find the spirit within yourself and look for it in others no matter what the outer behavior, and perhaps there is a chance that that spirit will respond to yours.

I remember well, what you said, "from the day I came into the world my destiny was leading me toward you." I'm sure you are right. I could be the catalyst to help you throw off the outer coverings of violence and anger which is not really you and bring out what has been waiting, hidden, inside. "Like bringing it forth as the sculptor does, so will you bring forth your courage and goodness and love." It is truly your poem. And, of course, we had to meet because we are companions. What is happening between us is definitely ours and yes, no one else would do. Our love is a magic which has been going on for a very long time. We know we can truly be ourselves with each other, and there will always be love and understanding and *never* criticism.

I can think of nothing better for you than what you are doing. I am glad you have the strength to stand your ground. I say again that the best defense in this difficult situation is to keep working on yourself.

Much, much love, dearest,
Ruth/Mom

January 26, 1990

Dear wonderful darling,

The nature books I've been sending you certainly teach us much. I knew you would like them, but I didn't realize how much.

Your letter of the twenty-first came, telling me of the barbarism of man. Of course you are disturbed, as I am. We must try to get this material published for others to see what goes on in our country, and hope enough will care enough to make some changes.

The doctor does, indeed, appear to be a very disturbed person. You say you might have made efforts to help the prisoner if it were possible. I wonder if it would have helped or made things worse?? That is one of the mysteries that we need to learn about and understand—what is the best thing, especially when each experience is different. I suppose we must pray, first of all, that we learn to hear the angels in order to find out what is best. I realize how scary your present situation is, and the fear of losing your self-esteem, but fighting back, even emotionally, with anger and violence, could be more weakening than strengthening in the end. The most effective thing is separating yourself from it—of course, the most difficult. To stand by and have to watch senseless cruelty and feel so helpless, that is what they deliberately play on. It can have a very destructive effect on those watching, destructive and debilitating. Gandhi had to watch much of that and still love everybody, and still understand that the cruel one is also a victim. I know how hard it is. One day you may have to watch it without restraints and that will be the real test.

A friend gave me a book about nature by a man from Australia who communicates with all of nature, including rocks and rivers — *Talking With Nature* by Michael Roads. I know it will mean much to you, and I have written to the publisher to ask permission to copy parts of it for you.

I embrace you with love and light and strength and endurance and all those good things. I love you in so many ways, and without reservations. That's all for now, my love, my beautiful son.

With much love,
Ruth/Mom

January 29, 1990

My darling,

Some beautiful little birds have been chirping outside my window all day. I have stopped my reading and have been listening for a while. I have never heard birds sound more beautiful. I get very special feelings from this beautiful day, knowing it is your birthday. To this day I give special reverence in celebration of the day you were born. Happy Birthday, Dear Mother, and God bless you.

I cannot help but keep commenting on, and complimenting *Kinship With All Life*. I am learning that the more I learn about other life forms and the part they play in the universal scheme of things, this knowledge seems to bring on a natural flow of love and an in-depth sense of appreciation which was formerly lost through ignorance. I am thoroughly amazed at the great harm man commits when he mentally separates himself from other universal life forms and proclaims himself master over all. All of the material you send me opens my eyes more and more, and I love it. It seems that the more I learn about real truth and the laws of oneness, the more liberated I feel in body, mind, and spirit. Sometimes I experience a beautiful feeling of total peace and unity, love and contentment with everything and everyone that I can think of. Then, as soon as someone says something to me or one of the guards comes to my door for whatever reason, this cosmic connection is broken and an invisible shield goes up.

I was allowed to participate in the outside recreation period today, so I went outside with the other guys for about two hours. The recreational yard is a small, fenced-in area about twenty feet wide and thirty feet long. It has a small basketball goal and a hundred and twenty pounds of weights that are permanently welded to the weight bar to keep guys from using them as weapons. A few of us played basketball, sat around and talked, and enjoyed the feeling of being outside in the sun.

To Mom, with love,
Martin

January 30, 1990

My dearest Martin,

Thanks for a lovely birthday greeting, which you timed just right to arrive on my birthday. I love your poem, the rose and the love they express.

I am thinking about nature and how good it is to have someone to talk to about it. Just think of how plants and insects are closely related to each other and are, in fact, dependent on one another. A great thought that came to me was that they would have had to be designed in that way. I used to wonder just where insects belonged in the order of things, and I could not accept that they were part of the animal world. Then, in my reading, I came across the idea that they belonged to the plant world, and I could say, "But of course." They were created as one being and the plant part is attached to earth, while the insect part is freed for movement and flight. And that is no more mysterious or remarkable than any other of God's wonderful creations.

And then I thought about how people, through their God-given ability to think and reason have the possibility, unlike other forms of life, of freedom and choice, and the ability to create. We can decide what we will do, how we will live, what we will become, within the limits of God's design, of course. Thinking is a form of flight. It can leave the body (or your prison cell) and go anywhere it likes in the universe. How little we appreciate this gift and either do not use it or misuse it. How patient God is with us. How appropriate your idea of the prodigal son who has gone astray. It can help us to be able to love our brethren and to find God's creation still resident in everyone.

We must learn to be a help to one another. How much we all do that is not in keeping with this! Slowly we learn how to do it better, and then we can become the best that it is possible to be. Humans have the semblance of having been freed of God and of one another, but not really, for we are all dependent on each other. And how much we affect each other! What a responsibility! Imagine God being dependent on us? Oy vey! Well, he is the one who started the whole thing, after all.

God bless you, dear son,
Ruth

February 5, 1990

Darling Ruth,

It's a beautiful feeling not to experience the blind rages of anger as much as I used to. Now that I am beginning to know myself better, I realize that I have actually been cultivating and nourishing my anger as if it were a part of me that I was afraid to lose. It is still not an easy thing to discard, because, as you say, "Before it can be truly eradicated and replaced with more pleasant emotions, it will keep coming back and have to be dealt with over and over." Despite the subtle and recurring forces of anger, I am much better than I was—miraculously so.

I am sure that if I had had the chance to help the prisoner who was beaten by the guards, it would have only made things worse because I was entertaining violent thoughts. Yes, prayer would have been more appropriate, my dear mother, but this would have been another one of those times when my emotions would have been governing my actions, and another mistake on my part. I can see how it would have been appropriate, also, to pray for the guards. I can see the event as a great learning experience for me in the sense that it gave me a chance to study myself and my reactions when faced with a situation of this kind.

The guy that was beaten is presently all right. He lives about five doors down from my room. We sometimes talk about different things, but not for very long because we have to talk at the top of our voices to hear one another and it is against the rules to talk too loud. He is about six-two, a hundred and eighty-five pounds, a little darker than I am, and with a mouth full of gold teeth. He is one of the guys who witnessed the incident between me and the guards at the other institution. I was not sure of this until he described the incident in great detail.

You know something, Mom (I feel really comfortable saying it), most of the time I am thoroughly convinced that you know me better than I know myself. Sometimes after reading your letters and the material you send me, I am so moved that I have to stand in awe. The love and purity that comes with them seems to wash away the deep loneliness, sadness, and pain that comes over me sometimes in this environment. I am not complaining because I know that these things are a part of reality and that they serve a divine and beautiful purpose, as you are teaching me so well. Therefore I am thankful for them. What I am trying to say is that I love and appreciate you so very, very much, and even though words often fall short when expressing my love, I will forever keep trying to give you, God, and the world, my best.

To Mom, with love,
Martin

February 9, 1990

My dear son,

I love the smiling whales on your envelope. The one going in the opposite direction must be you, going upstream when everyone else is going down. They are large and powerful and gentle creatures. God did good when he invented them. You know what is a good exercise—it is to meditate on various living beings, their gestures, movements, shape, size, what and how they eat, and anything you can think of about them. We learn much about the world in that way. It is another area where words cannot in any way express it. Through exercises such as this, one lives into the world in a living way and comes to understand it and to see the work of the creator. It can be a kind of recognition of individualization within the oneness.

Actually, although plants are fastened to earth, they, too, have some limited movement. One can see it in time pictures—of swaying and what looks like struggling upward and outward. I suppose all life must put out effort. And that is a nice thought. One can also see it in the way some plants follow the sun throughout the day.

I pray that it can become a regular event for you to go out into the air again.

Although it is early for your birthday, I am sending a card that I made especially for you. Some of it is traced, some is my own poor drawing. Here is what it says, and what it represents: "Happy birthday, dear son, friend, love, co-student, co-worker in the realm of spirit." The knight in armor is you, of course; the armor is the protection one needs in the world. The sword is to cut through the nonsense, falsity, untruth. The horse is the steed that carries you through and past all obstacles. I wanted for you a white rose—it came out a mix, perhaps correct? The snake is the coiled wisdom you have inside you that must slowly emerge, shedding skin after skin as you grow and change and overcome old conditioning and patterns. The baby, enwrapped—goodness, innocence, purity (as also the rose). The angel is to bless and watch over you; the eagle for flight and freedom; the lion, strength, courage. The tree is your love of nature, uprightness, strong roots in the earth of reality. The book is the knowledge which you gather every day of your life as you ask questions and find answers. The sun shines on you and all that you do and experience. The candle is the light that shines in darkness. Christ is with you in the form of the cross, and the star is representative of our beautiful, starry world and the heavens above. Your path is verdant green, strewn with flowers. The rocks are the obstacles that you will overcome. The face is me, your companion. I added a bull for steadiness, determination, endurance. The whole is permeated with love.

This is your birthday of entering the physical earth. There is another birthday of August 8, 1988, which is the beginning of your transformation into greater consciousness.

God bless and look after you.

Much, much love, my darling,
Ruth/Mom

———

February 13, 1990

My darling Ruth,

Your beautiful, inspiring and spiritually profound Happy Birthday letter/card arrived yesterday evening. Wow! What a beautiful card! There is something you said that hit me like thunder. In your words: "This is your birthday of entering the physical earth. There is another birthday of August 8, 1988. That is the beginning of your transformation into greater consciousness." I am sure that these are the most beautiful and meaningful words that can be said to another person. This is a card that I shall preserve as long as possible, and in my times of troubles and unsteadiness, I will look upon it for guidance and strength. Never have I had a more beautiful gift of pictures and words that complement each other. I thank you dearly, my dearest one.

I think security has decided that I am eligible to start going outside again on a weekly basis with the rest of the guys. We have just come back from a two-hour recreational period. The air outside feels great and everyone seemed to have a good time. It felt fresh and like a healthy dose of oxygen going into the lungs. It has really done me a lot of good because my thoughts are a lot clearer.

I hope you will always let me know how you are and when you are not feeling well. Every night before I go to bed I ask the Higher Ones to keep you safe and as comfortable as possible, and then I follow your good example and leave it in their hands. I feel that if I could be blessed with a portion of your strength, I would be able to carry others as you so lovingly carry me without the least complaint.

No, they do not allow prisoners to be present while they are searching the cells. It really doesn't matter if a person has a weapon inside his cell or not, because if the guards want you bad enough, they will find a weapon if they have to put one there themselves. Thanks to your prodding questions, I have long ago realized that the guards are no more vicious or cruel than the prisoners. The prisoners are known for their back stabbing and treachery toward one another. It seems it is just a matter of who has the power and authority over whom. During the search of my cell, they only destroyed my set-up. The thing that was supposed to disturb me the most was the way they threw my letters all over the floor. The incident did indeed disturb me, but not in the way they expected. After doing the meditation exercises that you gave me for my anger, I sat quietly while the anger and other emotions ran their course. Then came a deep sense of appreciation and understanding of the situation as a whole.

Love you so much,
Martin

February 15, 1990

Dearest Martin,

Here is some material I came across on the Bill of Rights. I did not know that Mr. Roosevelt had designated December 15 as Bill of Rights Day. I like his quote, "Those who have long enjoyed such privileges as we enjoy forget in time that men have died to win them." Evidently we can never take these rights for granted but must continue to fight for them every day. It is a sad thing that there is so much that requires that we protect ourselves, even from our government.

I awoke with all kinds of inspired ideas, and they have flitted away. And even now thoughts are coming and going as if they were butterflies, teasing me, but not letting me take hold of any. Normally that is fine, but unless I can capture an idea and put it down in words on paper, how can I share it with you?

Do not expect to ever completely get over fear. Fear just naturally wells up when one senses danger. We are filled with memories of things that have hurt, and it is surely a protective instinct. It is what we do when the fear wells up that makes the difference. At that point we can learn to use reason and not strike out blindly. Yet there are certainly times when we need to protect ourselves, and possibly other times when we can simply walk away. And there are times when we imagine the fearful thing, and it is not there at all.

I feel I should remind you to be always watchful in dealing with all people there. No matter how much loving you might be doing you cannot be sure what the other person might do or think. You are in a place where violence can happen at any time—like being in a war zone or an incendiary place. Take care of my boy!

I like what you say and say it back—

I love you dearly, greatly and very much,
Ruth/Mom

February 27, 1990

My precious darling,

Sometimes I find myself staring out of my window, wondering how a person could make such an impact on another's life, especially from so very far away. And then the voices of the angels speak. They say: "She's much closer than you realize, for there is not a day that goes by that you do not think of her with tender love and affection. As you are beginning to reach out to others, it is she who is always in the background of your thoughts, serving as a positive force and propeller. When you look upon the world now, with more understanding, it is she who is in the thoughts that form your gentle smile. In the times that you think you are alone, it is she who surfaces in your heart to warm and comfort you and to say, 'I am with you always.' " As I keep looking out of my window, I realize that thoughts such as these are endless when I am thinking of you. Yes, my darling, you are always here with me. For this night, I just want to say I love you.

Martin

———

March 6, 1990

Darling Ruth,

I was moved from one wing to another yesterday. The reason was because I felt it was necessary to hurt another prisoner on the recreation yard. It might, perhaps, have been avoided, but too many people wanted to see it happen, especially the guards. It had been building up for a couple of weeks, ever since the other person was placed next door to me. I would like to think that the incident just happened, but it could well have been an orchestrated plan by others to see me get hurt. As much as I can ascertain, the other person has already stabbed three people within the last year or so. He also appears to be psychologically unstable.

The incident started over him telling one of the guards that I was mistakenly receiving his mail. The guard evidently handled it too lightly because he kept insisting that I was being given his mail. After going out of my way to convince him that he was mistaken, he found something else to get my attention with. He started telling his friends that I was a homosexual, whom he once knew in population. Even though I have never been in general population at this prison, this type of rumor can cause a lot of trouble. Some of the prisoners who know me quite well tried to tell him that he was mistaken. He refused to hear of it and even stopped talking to the people who were trying to show him his mistake.

For two weeks I accepted the situation as calmly as possible. I tried to understand him and to talk to him, but it only seemed to make matters worse. I asked the Higher Ones for guidance and I feel they did, and still do, respond. I also realize that a man must do some things for himself, and that's what I did yesterday. It was not out of malice or dislike, but rather the only defense I could think of at the moment to keep him from hurting me, which I felt sure he intended to do. I considered not going to recreation, but that would be viewed as a cowardly act by others and would have caused problems in the future. I thought of taking the problem to the guards, but in this environment it is healthier to be thought of as dangerous rather than a coward and a weakling. Besides the guards were already aware of the problem and could very well have been part of it.

After being released into the recreation yard, I began to walk toward the basketball, while hoping this guy had come to his senses. The security guards and the coach heard him making threats but refused to do anything about it. Their behavior made me think that the whole thing was a plot. When he started walking behind me in a threatening manner, while calling me a lot of names, I knew that there was only one thing that would satisfy him for the moment, so I gave it to him. The struggle lasted probably less than thirty seconds and the guards just stood there and watched until the guy was knocked unconscious. They made a great show of being concerned after it was over. I was taken off of the recreation yard by an army of guards. This man is about six feet tall and about one hundred and sixty pounds. He seems almost fragile in appearance, but his attitude is extremely hostile and violent.

Most of the immigrants who are in the American prisons came straight to this country from the prisons in other countries. Seemingly, their only solution to solving most of their problems is to kill. The officials know this better than anyone, and believe me, they have been known to use this knowledge to get other prisoners killed. In this case, I cannot say that it was so, but there are just too many things that the guards chose to overlook for me to think that they didn't have anything to do with what happened.

A few minutes after the incident they told me to pack my personal property because they were going to take me to another wing, and that's where I am now. They also gave me a disciplinary report for assault on another prisoner. I will be going to kangaroo court sometime next week for the assault charge. They will surely find me guilty, and then I will be going to a disciplinary confinement wing for about sixty to ninety days. Disciplinary confinement is a punishment cell where they take our property and privileges away.

I keep feeling that the guy had some kind of weapon. After knocking him out, I was in the process of searching him, and then I was suddenly tackled by the guards. A weapon would have proved the guards' direct involvement beyond a shadow of a doubt because all of our clothes and bodies are supposed to be searched thoroughly before coming out of our cells, thus making it impossible for a person to get or have a weapon without getting it from the guards.

The aftermath of the incident disturbed me more than the incident itself because some of the guards began acting very strange toward me. I was getting the same angry and hostile vibes from them that I got from the guards at the other prison after the incident with the guard there. They were acting as if I had assaulted another guard. The doctor rushed to my cell after the incident and told me that this was proof that I needed to be on medication because I was too violent. If I had been any less sure of myself, I would have readily agreed with him. He appeared to be so sure of himself. I told him that I could not agree with his reasoning.

I may be reading too much into this, but the guards seemed very disappointed at the outcome. What really saddens me is that the guy wasn't receptive enough to realize that I am not his enemy. When leaving the wing, I looked in his eyes and saw the naked hatred that he has for me.

I am praying for him, as well as myself, because I know that we are both in need of the help and guidance of the Higher Ones. I am also praying for the other ones like him and the

Martins of the world because I realize that we are many and one.

I thank you for being my very special companion.

With infinite love,
Martin

March 7, 1990

My dearest Ruth,

There is no doubt that I will be sending some of my books to you to save for me. When I go to court for the disciplinary write-up, all of my personal belongings will be taken away and sent to the property room until I am released from the punishment cell. The property room guards will do an inventory of my property, and at the same time, they will decide if I have too much stuff. If so, I will send it to you for safekeeping. Most of my property consists of the beautiful literature that you have sent me and this is what they will probably complain about. The knowledge that these books contain gives me a sense of completeness, security, and other feelings that are beyond the natural order. It fills a certain void within me that cannot be filled by anything else, and it gives meaning to the things that were formerly a mystery to me. These books have helped to release me from much personal anger, hatred, and ignorance. Yes, I wish to keep them as long as I live for further and more in-depth study. They are truly my most valued possessions. Books are a beautiful and ingenious way to pass on knowledge.

Please know that I do not consider the incident with the prisoner I had to hurt as a setback or failure. It saddens me greatly, because I do not like reverting to violence, but it seems that some people understand little else.

To Mom, lovingly,
Martin

March 10, 1990

My darling Martin,

To most of the world my memories of our past would be considered a lot of nonsense. To me it is very real. There are no words to describe the feelings of what we have been and still are to each other. But most important is the spiritual work that we set out to do very, very long ago, and for which we have been in training, not just in this life but over many centuries. Through your letters I know that you are aware of it too, and feel the same inner excitement at the task we are doing and that we will surely one day do together.

Sometimes I feel your impatience at getting on with it—an impatience I share with you. We have worked at different things, of course, so that together we will be a greater whole. We are male and female so that in that way, too, we balance and complement each other. You are amazingly ready to take and work with my suggestions, testing them for yourself without the hindrance of the lower ego, because you know, as do I, that knowledge, understanding, and wisdom far surpass anything else we can strive for on earth. We can also, of course, include love, goodness, caring for the earth and all on it, appreciating beauty.

I reach out across the miles to grasp your hands, to embrace you, to express love from overflowing heart. We meet in the name of Christ.

The publisher of the nature book, from which I wanted to copy parts for you, has offered, instead, to send you a copy of the book. That is very dear and I have already sent him a thank you letter. I know it will be very meaningful to you.

I love you,
Ruth

———————

March 10—Evening

My dear darling,

I have your letter about the latest incident. Evidently the guards do not give up on trying to have you killed. It does seem to have been staged, as if letting you out on the recreation yard had a purpose. There were too many things happening in a way that could hardly be just coincidence.

Because man has a mind, and because he has the possibility of becoming a truly free being in the way I have already spoken to you about, he can also become more beastly than the animals who are still governed by instinct, by hunger and need. But man can be utterly cruel. There are people without conscience and there is such a thing as evil. It is quite possible that the love we work for cannot reach them. I have never been able to come to real answers regarding this, only questions. It's a bit different from what Starr Daily had to deal with, for I have the sense that he dealt with ignorance but not with deliberate evil. This is something we still have to find out about, and our prayers for guidance and understanding are the only tools we know of. That you pray for this man and the guards and the doctors is also important. Me, too. I pray for you all.

Know that although this saddens me very much, I am taking it well. It changes one thing in my thinking. I had hoped in my heart (like a mother) that all would go uphill and that it would be possible for you to work for a parole. Now I know that I may not harbor any wishes at all. Everything has to be left entirely in God's hands and in that of his helping angels. What, then, are the things we may ask for and hope for? All I can think of is to ever grow and to be the best that we can be. I think of how much I have to be grateful for. Mostly I am grateful for you and for our love.

I am so glad that you could be clear enough in yourself to refuse the doctor's drugs. How quickly he was there to offer them—the great panacea for everything—take away the individual's consciousness and independence.

I have no special feeling about the thing that happened, what it might mean. I only have trust in you and in your striving and sincerity. I see no evidence of anger in you but of self-defense. I do not see it as assault, and as I said before, things should be called by their right names.

I have been working on this letter on and off for several hours. I think I am a little numb, but I truly have no fear or anxiety and that even surprises me. It could well have been a situation in which you were guided and perhaps it is part of the training. I do have trust in God's guidance and in you, my son.

March 11—

I awoke this morning thinking about the events you wrote about—the psychopath put in the cell next to yours, the fact that he has done several stabbings and is still taken out on the recreation yard, that he threatened you and was taken out with you, that he manages to get weapons in situations where it is impossible without the guards' cooperation, that they began to take you out just then, after not doing so for quite some time.

I am glad you are still alive, and I hope, with God's help that you will continue to remain so. You are learning about the worst aspects of people, and maybe it all has a good purpose. Only one person there seems to stand out as being caring—the elderly nurse you wrote about. How strong she must be to be able to withstand it. She sounds very special. I am glad she is there for you, even though she cannot do it openly. Except for her you are quite alone in that place. I look at you and feel good about you. It feels as though you are where you should be, doing what you must do, making progress, no matter what it may look like outwardly. I try to surround you with love and light and Christ's protection.

I love you, my beloved,
Ruth/Mom

March 12, 1990

My dearest Ruth,

I went to disciplinary court Friday, and they sentenced me to sixty days in the punishment cell, as I expected. If given a choice, I would have declined appearing at the hearing because the board was arbitrarily designed by the guards, for the guards, on the principle of "We may not always be right, but we are never wrong." When they asked me how did I plead, this was a moment that I could not control my wagging tongue. I told them that it was useless to plead to anything, since in the eyes of the Ku Klux Klan I would always be guilty by virtue of my blackness. After that they no longer felt it necessary to hide their hatred, which was apparent all the time.

Sometimes when thinking about it I have to laugh, because

at one point I was earnestly trying to alter my attitude to please and get along with a people who can only be satisfied with the passive side of me. I realize that it is not so much a race of people, or individuals, but rather a system—a system designed a long time ago by the beast (as you call it), and it has affected most people in a negative and sick way. To give you a better idea of what I am talking about: Though I was never taught this by anyone directly, until I met you, I was thinking that God did not particularly like blacks and that our skin color was evidence of this dislike.

So from the time that I woke up one day and realized that I was black, I began to unwittingly dislike my blackness. I was indirectly taught by whites and blacks alike to be ashamed of my black features and characteristics. I am sure that deep within me I have known better, but I was not consciously aware enough, and strong enough, to fight off the outer impressions of the world. Thus began my long, embittered, and frustrated battle against God and the world. And until I met you, I had been rebelling and striking out at a system in the only way I knew how.

Yes, there are black officials and black prisoners here who seem to hate my type of attitude and thinking, because I do not fit the pattern that they have succumbed to, that of the stereotypical black, who is only content with doing the bidding of the white master. Would you believe that there are blacks in the world who are willing to kill people like myself for some of the same reasons that the skin heads and the Ku Klux Klan are?

This is a paradox that I am not qualified to fully address, but I can personally vouch for its truth. I have seen and felt evidence of this all of my life, especially here and I am just beginning to understand it. I hope that I am making some kind of sense to you, because I'm not sure I understand it myself. I feel most certain that you don't mind, but I must ask you, anyway, if you mind that I talk about this kind of thing with you? I don't have anyone else that I can talk to about it but you, and it helps me to be honest about something that has been a plague to me all of my life. You see, I have found that most blacks are afraid to discuss this even in this day and time. They like to pretend that the problem does not exist. This is another part of "the great lie" that I cannot accept.

They have put me in the disciplinary confinement cell with

a few cosmetic items, a Bible, and the necessary items to write my letters with. I am now on a different wing. The food flaps are always locked, the glass parts of the doors have a steel screen and bars on the inside, and the cell window is the same. There is a lot of screaming between the prisoners most of the day in an effort to communicate with one another. There is also a lot of banging on the doors to get the guards' attention for writing materials and other needed items that can only be gotten by the guards. Most of the time the guards will intentionally ignore them, while the prisoners work themselves into a frenzy and do something stupid to bring punishment upon themselves. This is seemingly an everyday cycle. The most prevalent force here seems to be hatred, violence, and anger. I am forced to wonder what is the overall purpose of a system such as this. It is like the mad scientist who creates madness only to define his madness as sanity. Along with, and through the madness, there are profound lessons, as well, but only if we can shut off our personal likes and dislikes as they come to us from our surroundings.

My dearest mother, sister, friend, companion, teacher, and more, you have given me so very, very much in such a short period of time. It's like an instant transformation. There are so many things that I would like to share with you in person. There are so many beautiful things that I would like to say to you, but words often fail me when expressing our profound and unusual love.

Endless love,
Martin

————

March 14, 1990

My darling son, companion, friend,

This morning I am thinking about what your life has been like in this incarnation. I see it as of you having been dropped down into the deepest midst of a human jungle. I think of the years spent in prisons, of the frustration, anger, fighting to keep alive. With all my faith, and with my trust in you, I still cannot help feeling a few moments of anxiety about your present situation. Then I remind myself to look at the longer span of time—the many lives before this one, the many still to come, the deeper meaning of life, and the good that will come out of your present pain. Then I can remember the whole as a process and the present as a moment in time. Love fills me, and an appreciation of your beautiful soul.

Again and again pictures come of the years spent behind bars, of a childhood spent virtually alone, of emotional and physical pain. And I think of how many experience this in this mad, mad world. I do nothing with all these thoughts and feelings except to be aware of them and to respond with deep inward thoughtfulness and caring. At this moment there is no personal feeling—not even sadness—just seeing, and feeling the need, and knowing that we will be part of the change. Change must come over the long future; we will be part of it, and we will need all the patience we are learning now, for it will be a long, difficult process. And we will surely need something else that we are both learning about—the soul-consciousness that it is all one, one body, one universe, one God, interconnected, and that what we do to each other, to the world, to the smallest part of it, we do to the whole.

My love for you never stops and I try to enlarge it, to make it big enough to encompass the whole. And I try to know the whole, to tune in to the amazing, wonderful creation, and to love it without reservation, as I love you.

God bless and keep you,
Ruth/Mom

CHAPTER 13

Bringing Us Up to Date

As of this date, November 1991, I offer this brief account of some events that have taken place since March of 1990. I add, also, a few words about some of the conditions under which Martin presently lives.

Before his time was up in the punishment cell, someone evidently caught up with the judge's order, and Martin was suddenly whisked off to a mental hospital. There he was allowed to move about freely within the section where he was housed, which included a recreation room and a fenced outdoor area with gardens and trees. It was a great luxury for him to be able to be out of doors for a time each day. There the doctors again tried to push their mind-paralyzing drugs, which he was able to refuse. After a few months he was declared sane and was moved back to the prison for his trial.

At his mock trial, in an all-white courtroom, in front of the judge and jury, and while in painfully tight leg shackles, Martin was jumped by a number of guards and sheriffs (who afterward claimed he had struck his lawyer) and mercilessly beaten and choked almost to death. Conveniently, this time he had been taken to the courtroom only in leg shackles instead of the whole paraphernalia they usually put on him. One of them said to him during the beating, "Too bad you have on these shackles or we could kill you and claim you tried to escape."

It took the jury a few minutes to bring in a verdict of guilty, and he was given a life sentence. He is kept on the most maximum security wing of the most maximum security prison in the state.

He is occasionally reminded by the guards that they do not forget, and when some of their very stringent restrictions were recently eased (for example, he is now taken out of his cell with handcuffs only, with his hands behind his back), it was not a reason for rejoicing but only for further concern. It makes me wonder what new attack they may have in the works. Although there are very strict rules about prisoners being taken out of their cells only one at a time, there is another prisoner there who constantly threatens to kill him. He claims to be a spiritual student, yet he has remarked that there is nothing wrong with killing, since you only kill the physical body.

If they have their way, he will spend the rest of his life in this airless cell, and who knows how long (or short) that life might be? His unforgivable crime—to defend himself from attack by a guard who was known to regularly beat up prisoners while they were in shackles, and who had previously sent Martin to the hospital with such a beating. This time he made the mistake of attacking the prisoner without the precaution of first having him handcuffed behind his back.

Martin's attempts to get an appeal are constantly sabotaged by the same lawyer appointed by the court to "represent him." They continue to play the library game. There must be some rule or law that makes it mandatory to allow inmates library privileges at certain times, because they periodically let him know that his library privileges have been reinstated. It takes several months to get a book to him and then, after the first book, they claim it has not been returned and the privileges are again withdrawn. The last notice that his library privileges had been canceled was signed by the same person who personally picked up the book directly from Martin.

They have just made new restrictions about books: Prisoners are no longer allowed to request them on their package permits. Books must now be ordered directly from a publisher or book dealer and paid for from the prisoner's own prison bank account. He must first request permission for each title on a special form, and *if* approved, he may then send his order and check. Prisoners are not permitted to receive donated books, magazines, or other literature. Loaning, trading, or borrowing of books between inmates is forbidden, and such materials are confiscated as contraband. Educational, religious, legal and medical books are forbidden. The above information is taken from an actual prison form.

We just went through a period when everything I sent to him, and to our other friend in another section of the same prison, was returned if anything at all, even a puzzle, was included with the letter. Two letters were not even opened.

That type of restriction seems to be over now. As our friend says, "Like children their attention span is short and they lose interest in their games, bless them. Sooner or later they will get silly again and you can withhold extras until it passes." Still, the amount of extras one can send is very limited, more than in the past when Martin and I first started writing

Prisoners are consistently provoked to get them to behave in such a way as to have their sentences extended, and one can only imagine that it must be intentional. After all, prisons are big business—and the bigger the better for them. The state where Martin is a prisoner gets top ranking for some of the highest rates of recidivism in the country. It is the taxpayer who supports this madness.

To prevent people from getting an education and from having access to good literature is about as serious a crime as anyone can commit toward another human being. Why is it permitted? When I wrote to a state legislator about the restrictions against education when the prisoner wants to do it on his own, when it would cost the state nothing, her reply was criticism of me. This from a black woman who, in not listening to such a thing, rejects her race and her feminism. I did not ask her to do anything, only to be aware of the situation. Prisoners are just as much in a slave situation as in the days when slavery was part of our way of life.

Listen My Son

Perhaps here, in the magic of poetry, one can embody what the letters express:

Listen My Son

I am thinking of you, my darling,
While quiet tears flow.
In inner eye I see the iron bars
Within which you live,
And am so aware of it
As commentary on our times.

I weep, not just for you, dear,
But for all the world,
For all those who
In one way or another,
Live within bars,
Often of their choosing.

Find freedom, beloved companion,
There behind prison bars,
Especially there,
Where outer monstrousness
Forces you to go within.
Only there true freedom lives.

Find peace, dear friend,
Find that which is the best of you.
Cultivate it—the love, the caring,
The giving from the heart.
Become a shining star
For all around you
Who are in pain.

Find joy, my precious one,
Just there, in the midst
Of violence, anger,
Hate, fear, and so much pain.

Even there find treasures
In little things of beauty,
In kindnesses, in thoughts profound.

Find humor, dearest,
Which is everywhere,
Especially in dark places.
Laugh at absurdities
Which men take
All too seriously.

Find love, beautiful son,
Let Christ's love, through you,
Shine forth to all in need,
And who is not?
Let light and love,
Peace, courage, hope,
Become your greatest,
Most earnest striving.

Bibliography

This is a limited list of just the titles mentioned in the book. There are many more that he loves as well. When people are astounded by Martin's ability to write so well, with so little education, I think it can be explained by his great love of books.

Chronicles of Narnia by C. S. Lewis. New York: Macmillan Child Group, 1970–1986 (seven books.)

Gandhi Autobiography by Mohandas K. Gandhi. New York: Dover, 1948–1983.

The Great Initiates (Hermes) by Edward Schuré. Sioux City, Iowa: St. George Press, 1961.

Kinship With All Life by J. Allen Boone. New York: Harper & Row, 1954.

Knowledge of the Higher Worlds and Its Attainment by Dr. Rudolf Steiner. Hudson, N.Y.: Anthroposophic Press, 1947.

The Little Prince by Antoine de Saint-Exupéry, translated by Katherine Woods. New York: Reynal, a division of Morrow, 1943.

The Long Walk by Slavomir Rawics. New York: Lyons & Burford, 1956–1984.

Love Can Open Prison Doors by Starr Daily, 1934. Presently out of print; photocopy available from Sunray Books c/o Element Books, Rockport, Mass.

The Notebooks of Paul Brunton, Volume I: *Perspectives* by Paul Brunton. Burdett, N.Y.: Larson Publications, 1984.

The Prophet by Kahlil Gibran. New York: Random, 1985.

Should It Make Sense? by Ruth Sanders. Rockport, Mass.: Sunray Books c/o Element Inc., 1987.

Siddhartha by Hermann Hesse. New York: New Directions/Bantam Books, 1951.

Space Trilogy Series by C. S. Lewis. Composed of *Out of the Silent Planet, Perelandra* and *That Hideous Strength*. New York: Macmillan, 1944–1946.

Talking With Nature by Michael Roads, Tiburon, Calif.: H. J. Kramer, Inc., 1987.

I Thought I Walked Alone—The Poems of Ruth Sanders, by Ruth Sanders. Rockport, Mass.: Sunray Books c/o Element Inc., 1990.
Winnie the Pooh by A. A. Milne. New York: Dutton, 1971.